DISCOVERING VENICE ITALY

La Serenissima

PICTORIAL SEARIES

Presented by

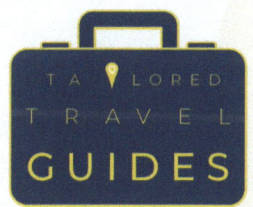

Discover your journey!

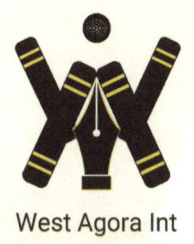

West Agora Int

a WEST AGORA INT S.R.L. Brand
www.tailoredtravelguides.com
Edited by WEST AGORA INT S.R.L.
WEST AGORA INT S.R.L. All Rights Reserved
Copyright © WEST AGORA INT S.R.L., 2023

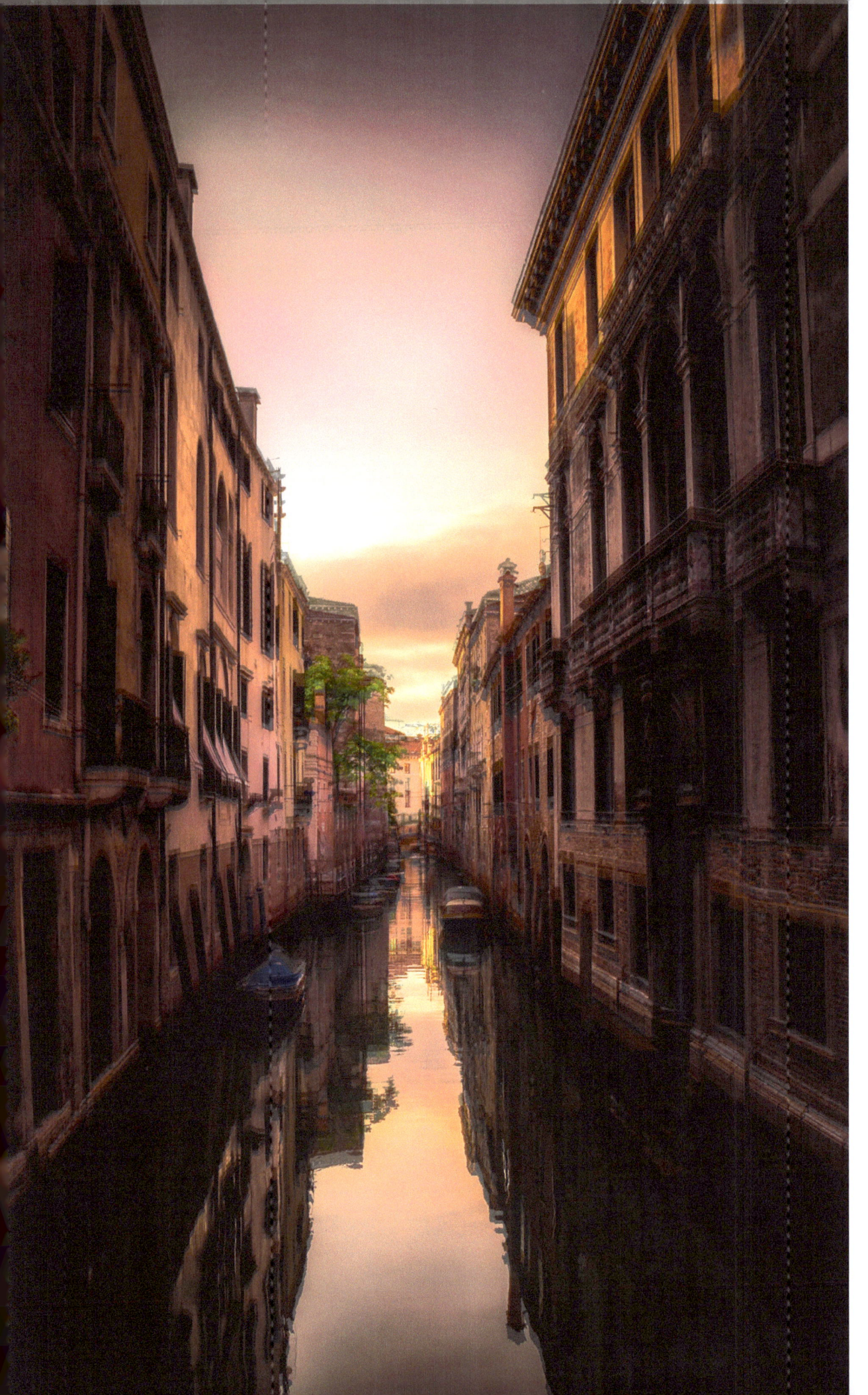

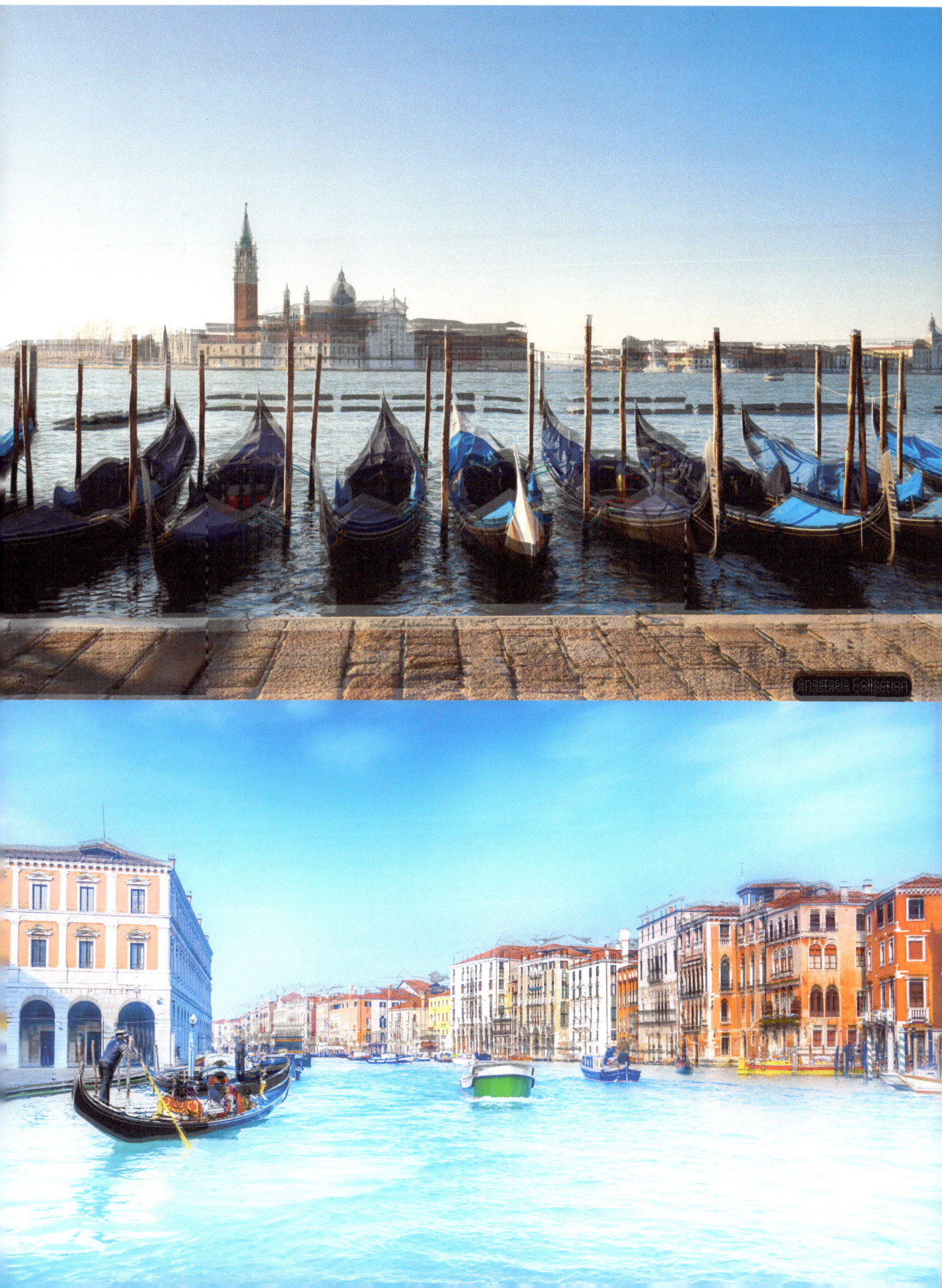

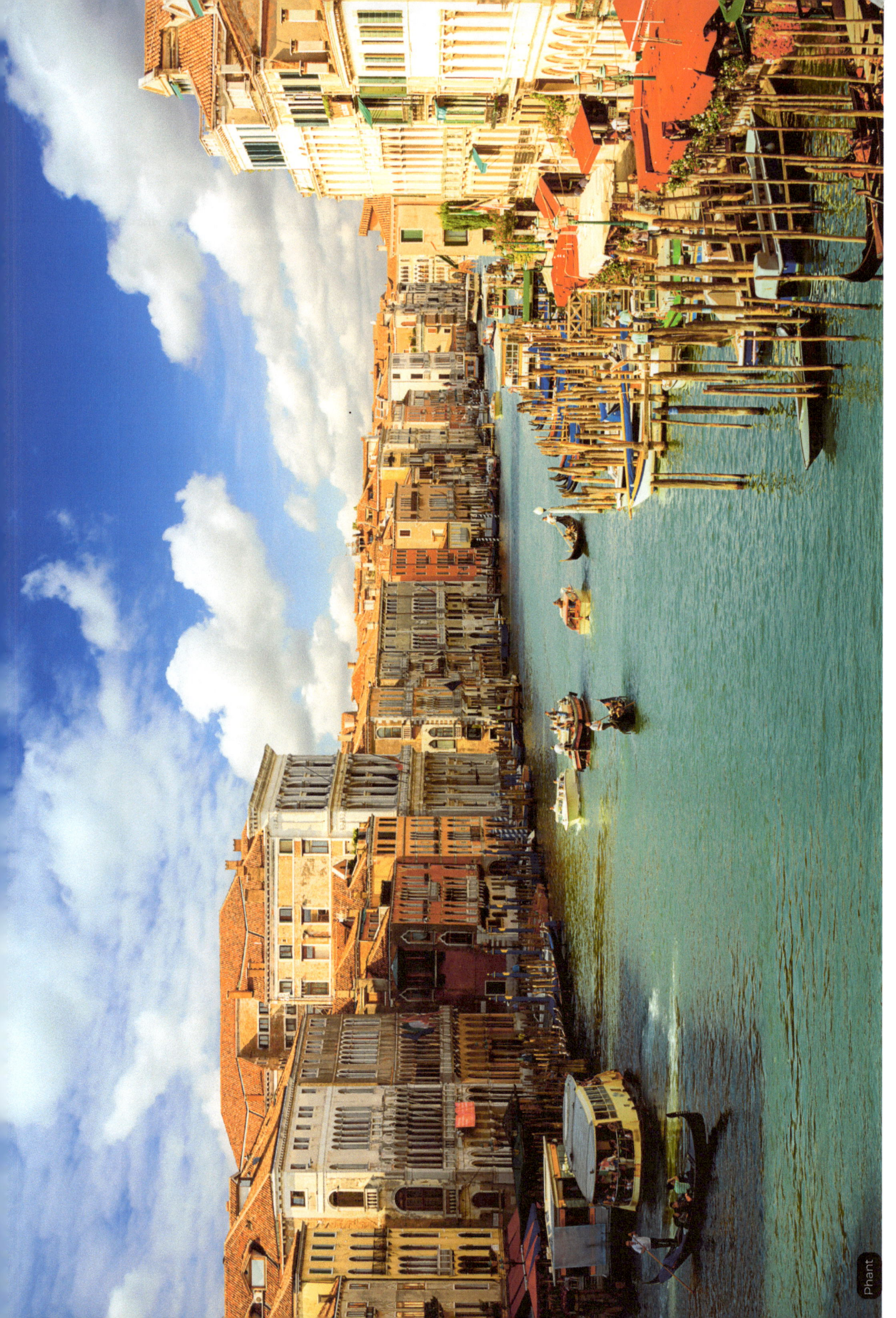

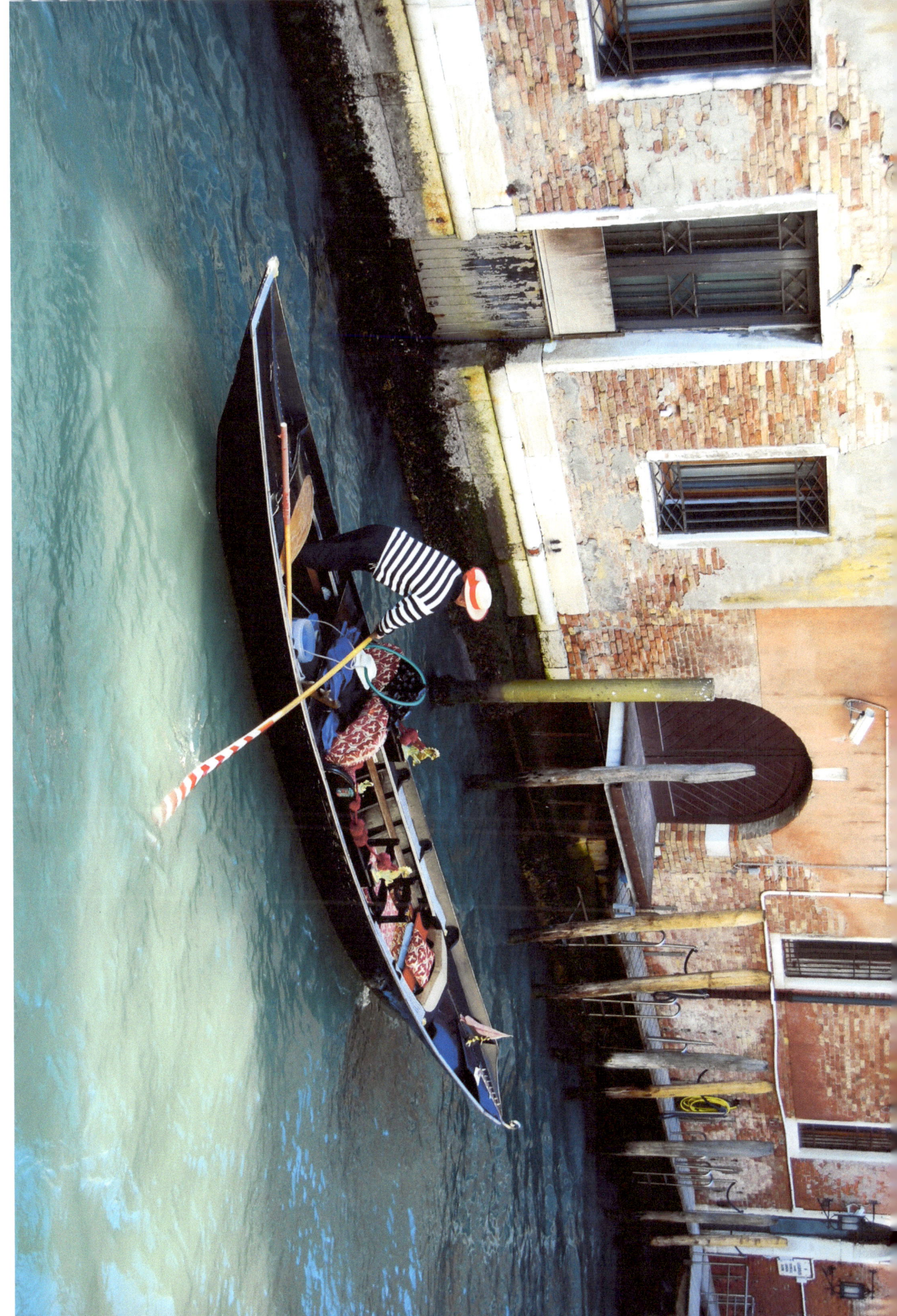

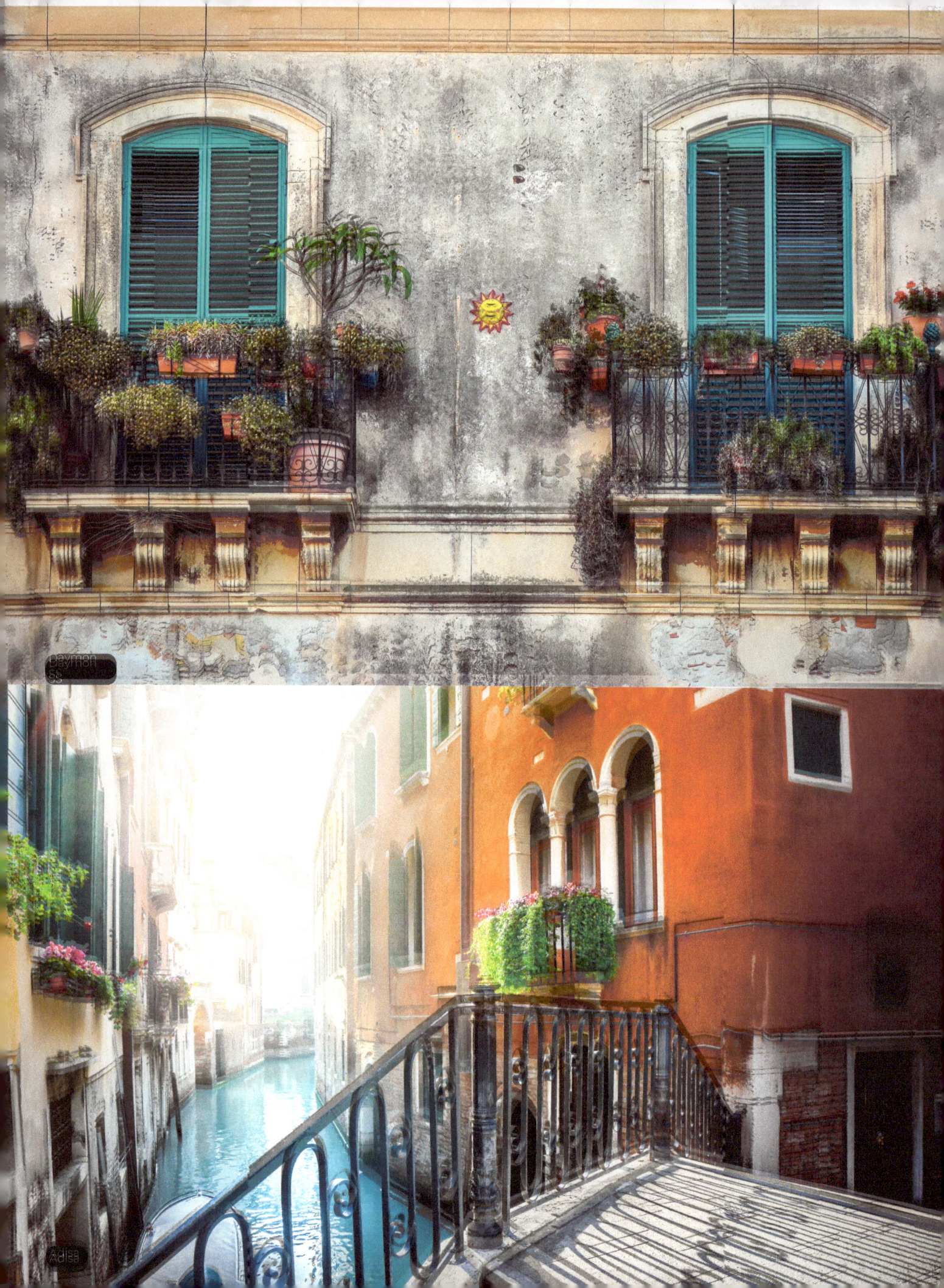

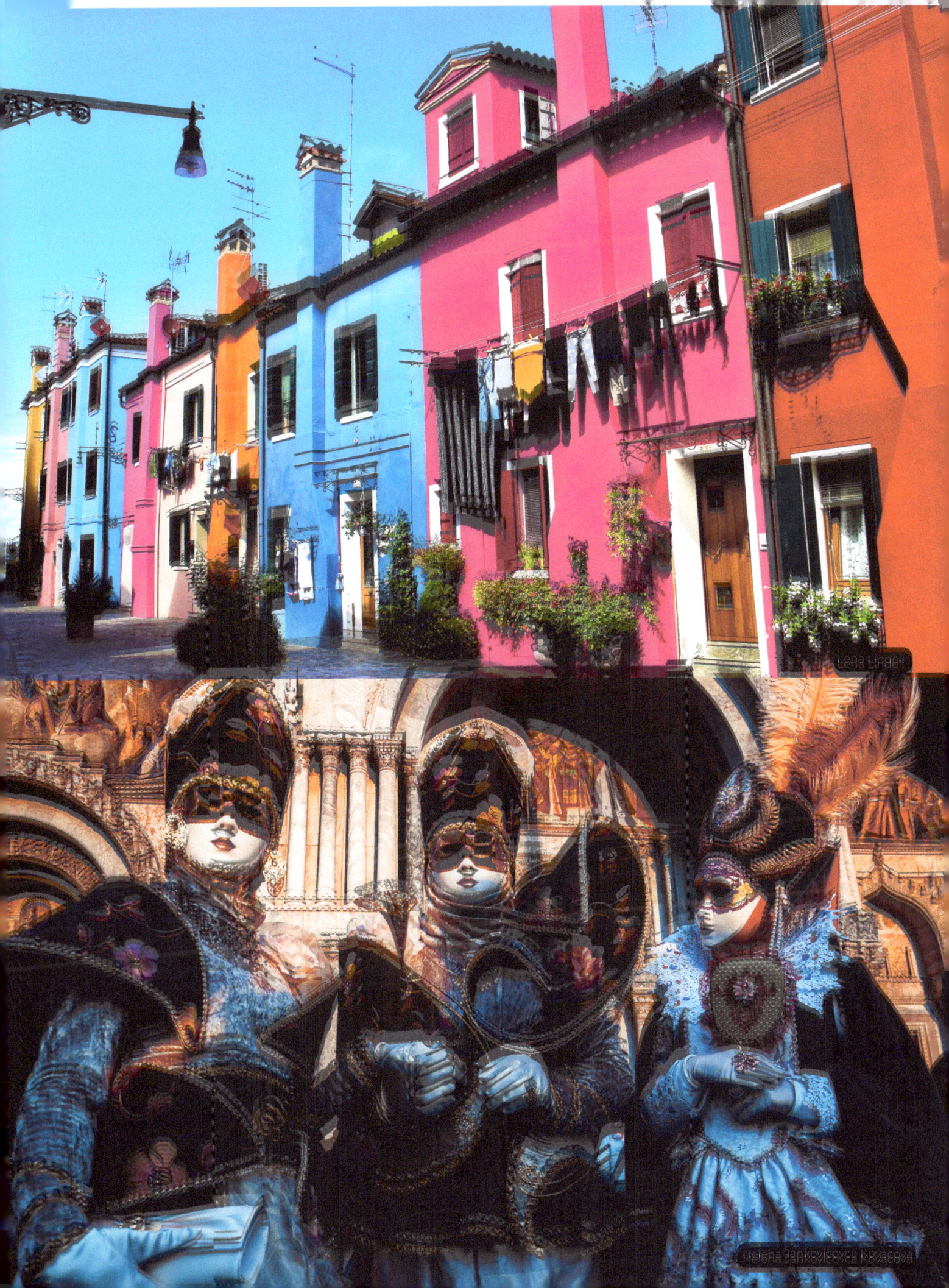

Basilica di San Marco

Nestled in the heart of Venice, the Basilica di San Marco stands as an awe-inspiring emblem of the city's rich history and artistic magnificence. Constructed in the 11th century, this architectural masterpiece showcases the unique blend of Byzantine, Western European, and Islamic influences, reflecting Venice's position as a historical crossroads of cultures.

As one approaches Piazza San Marco, the Basilica's opulent façade captivates the eye. Adorned with a symphony of gold mosaics, intricate carvings, and statues, it tells a story of Venice's glorious past. The five iconic domes, inspired by the Hagia Sophia in Constantinople, crown the Basilica, symbolizing Venice's power and influence in the medieval world.

Stepping inside, visitors are enveloped in a realm where art and devotion merge. The golden mosaics, covering more than 8,000 square meters, depict scenes from the Bible, transporting onlookers to a heavenly realm. The famed Pala d'Oro, an exquisite altarpiece adorned with precious gems, further exemplifies the Basilica's wealth and artistic patronage.

The Basilica di San Marco is not just a church; it is a testament to Venice's historical significance and a beacon of its enduring legacy. It invites travelers to explore the depths of a city where every stone whispers tales of opulence, faith, and artistry.

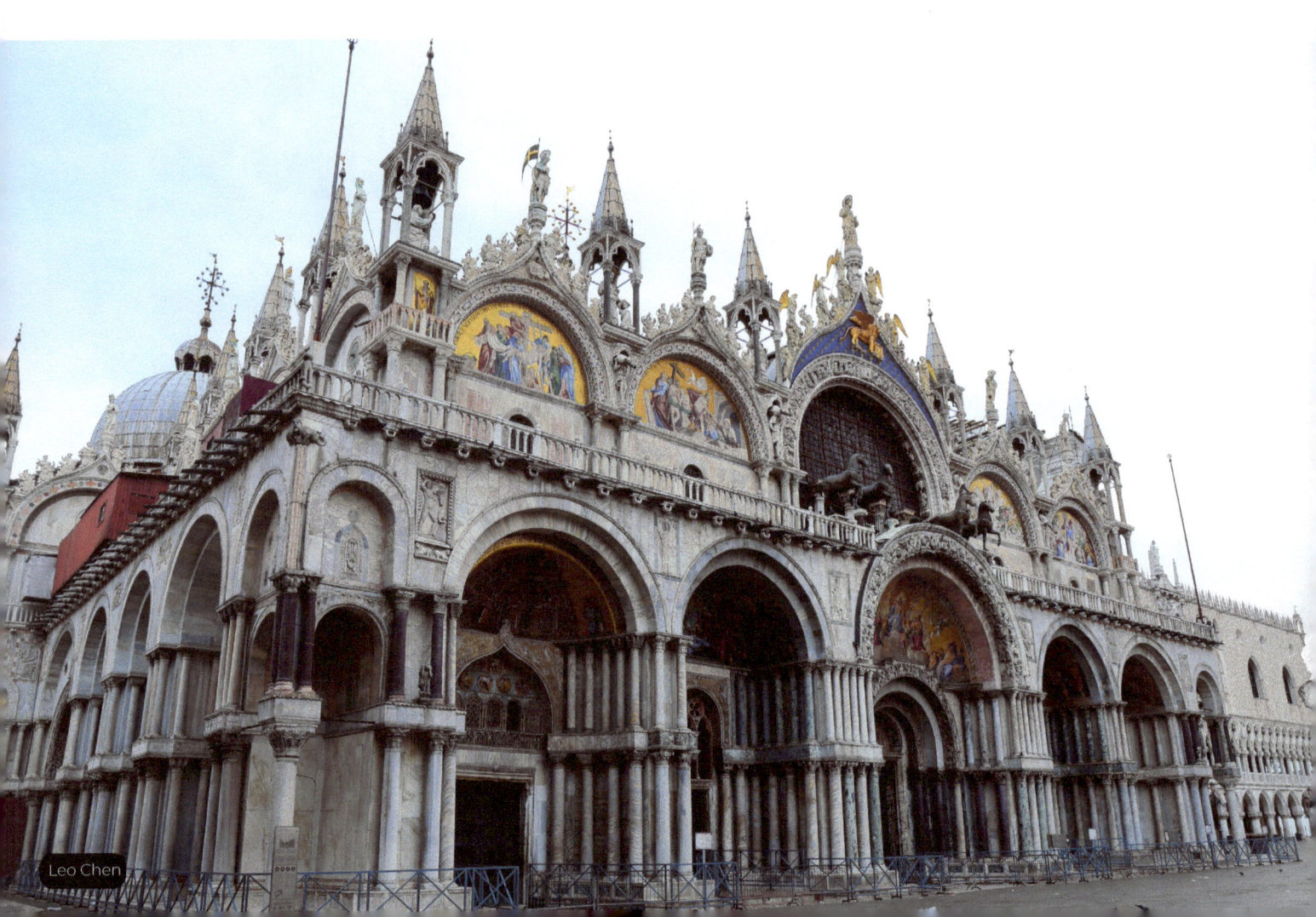

Leo Chen

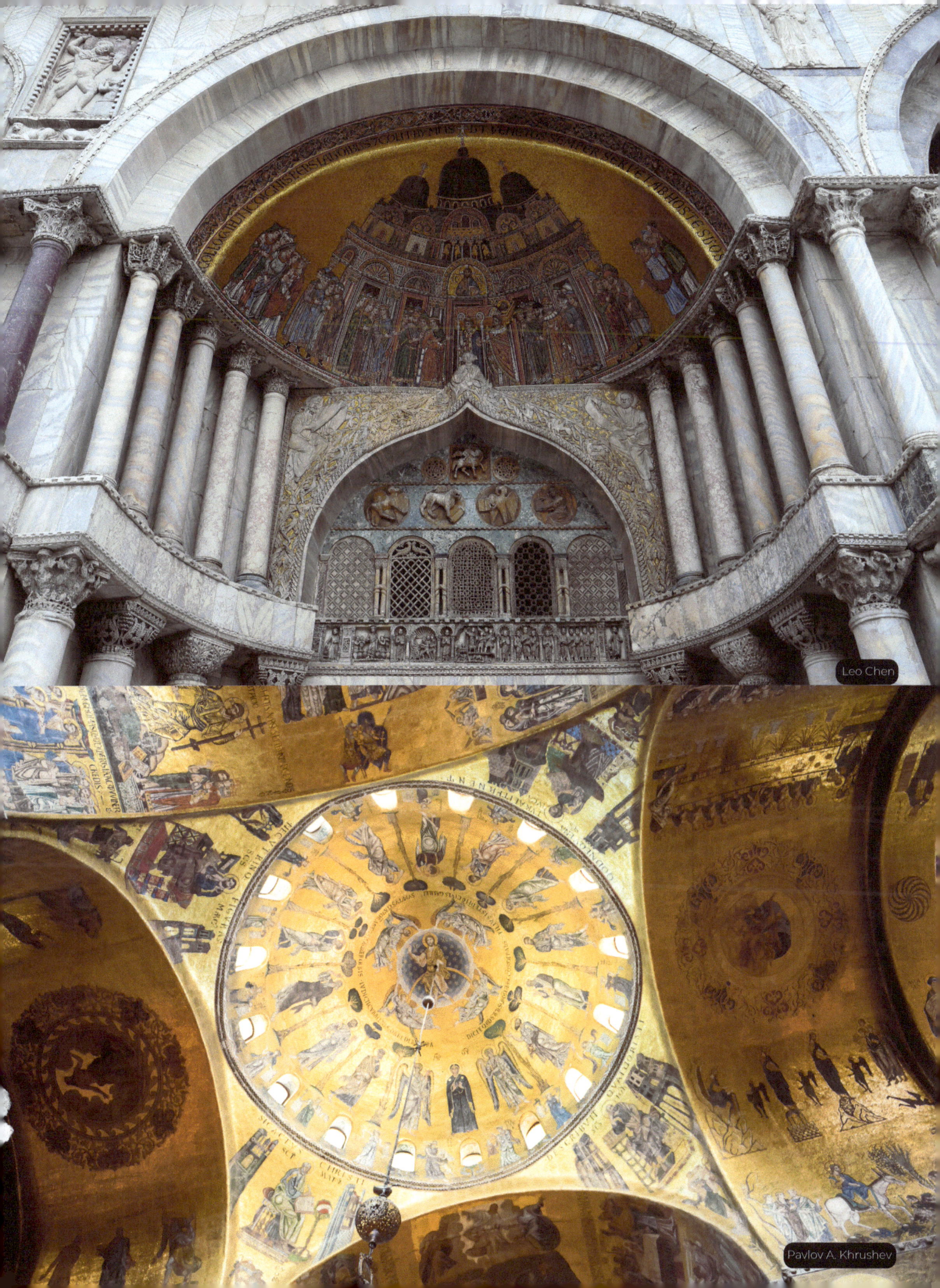

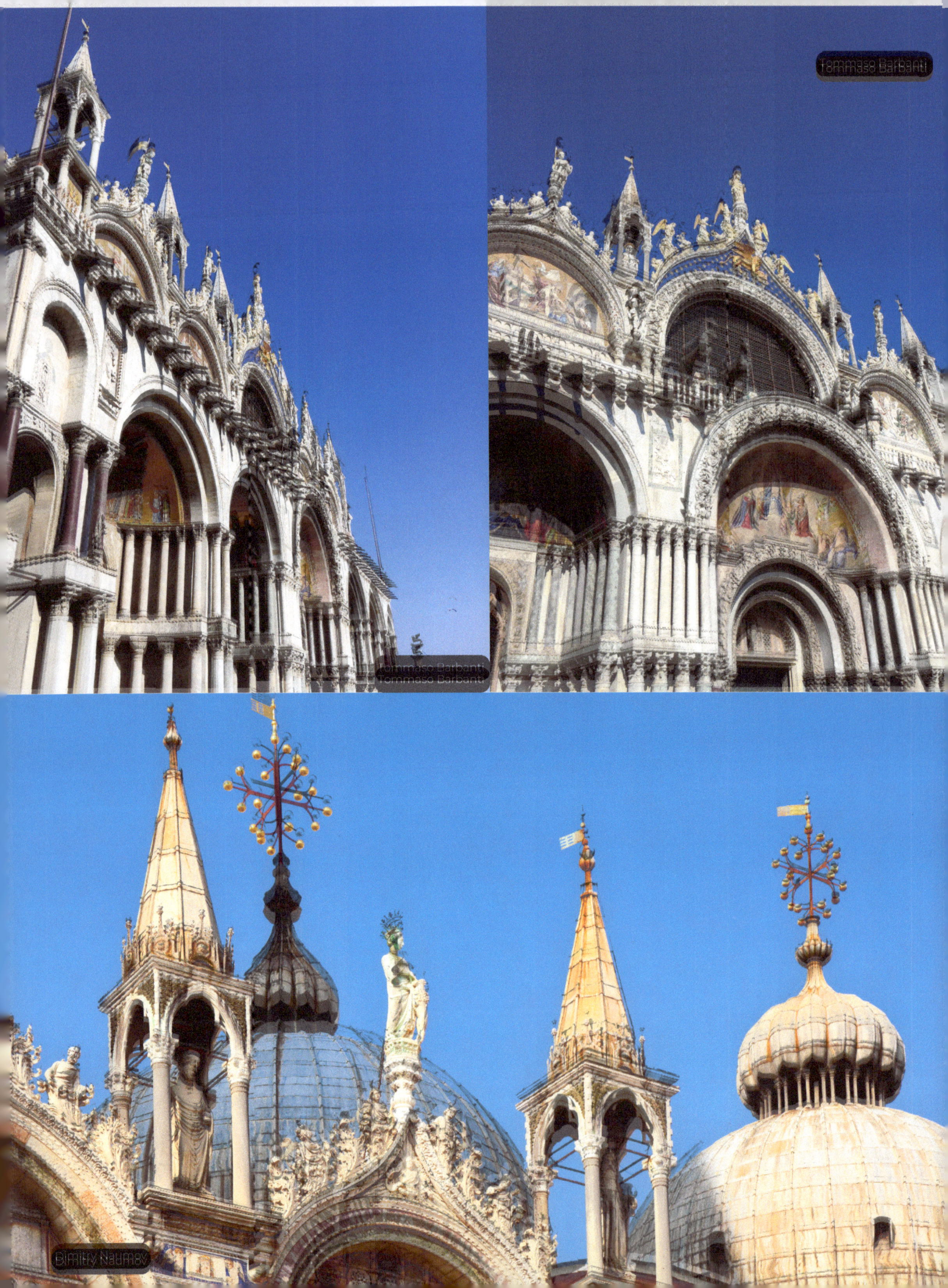

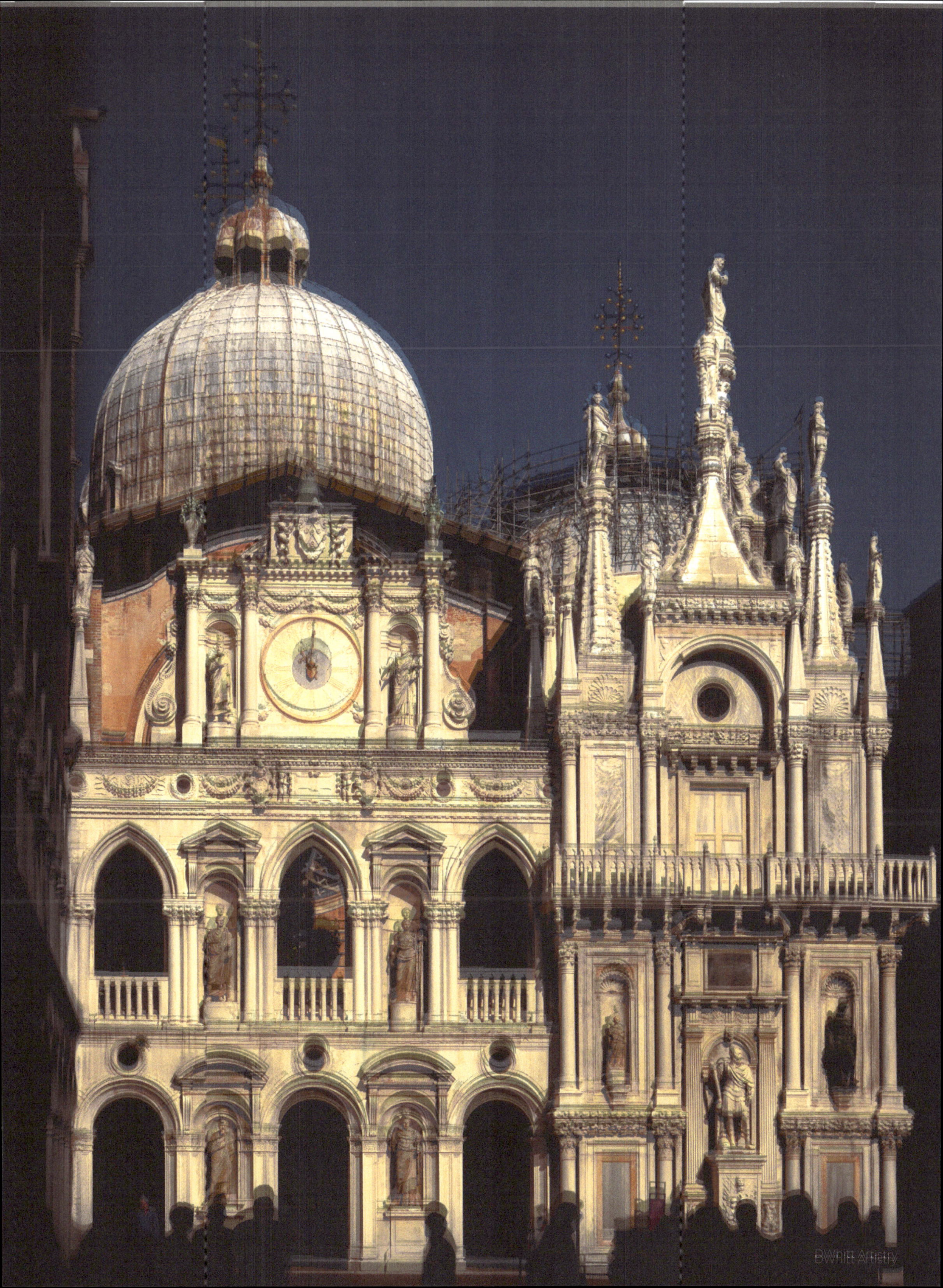

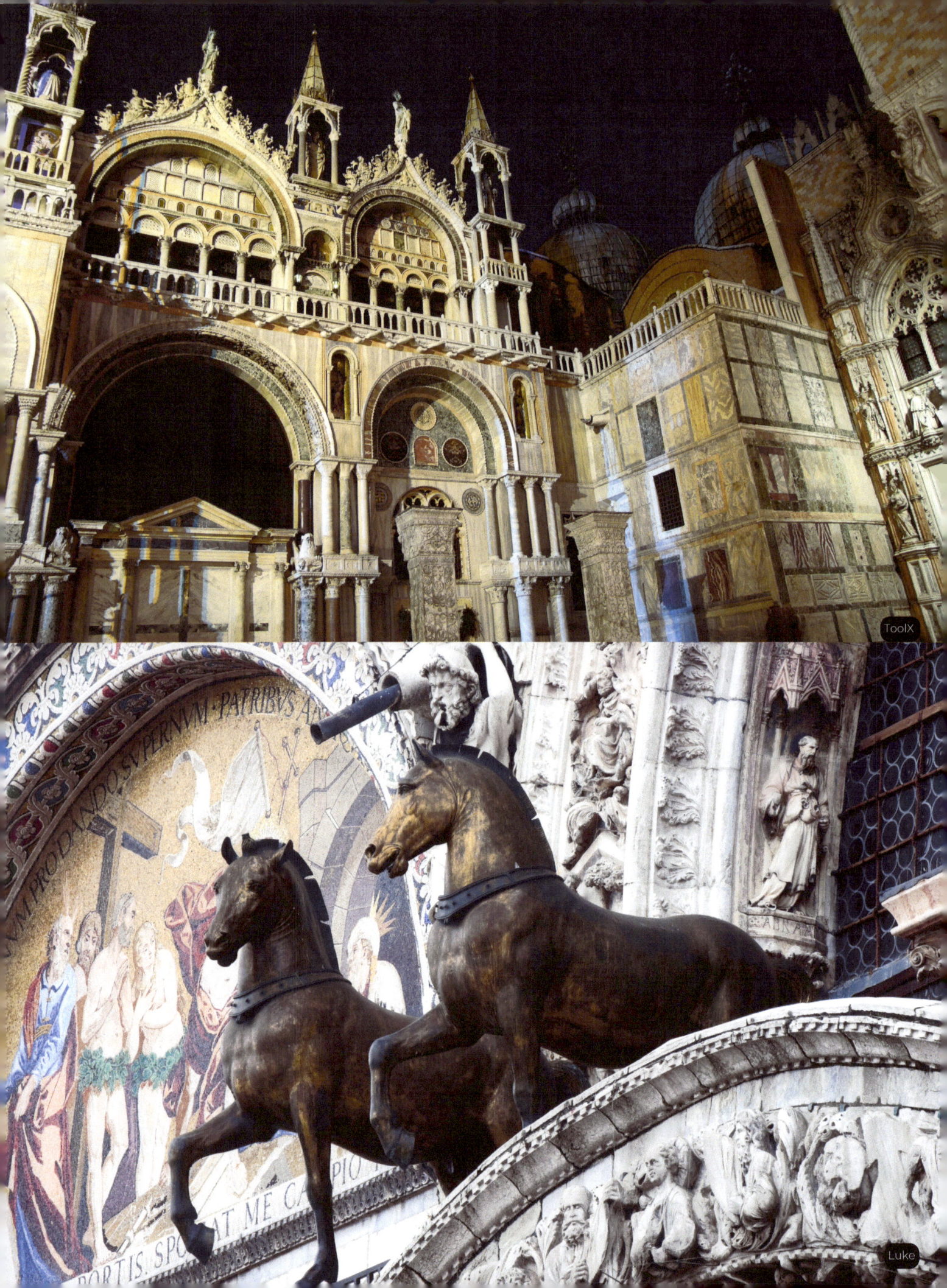

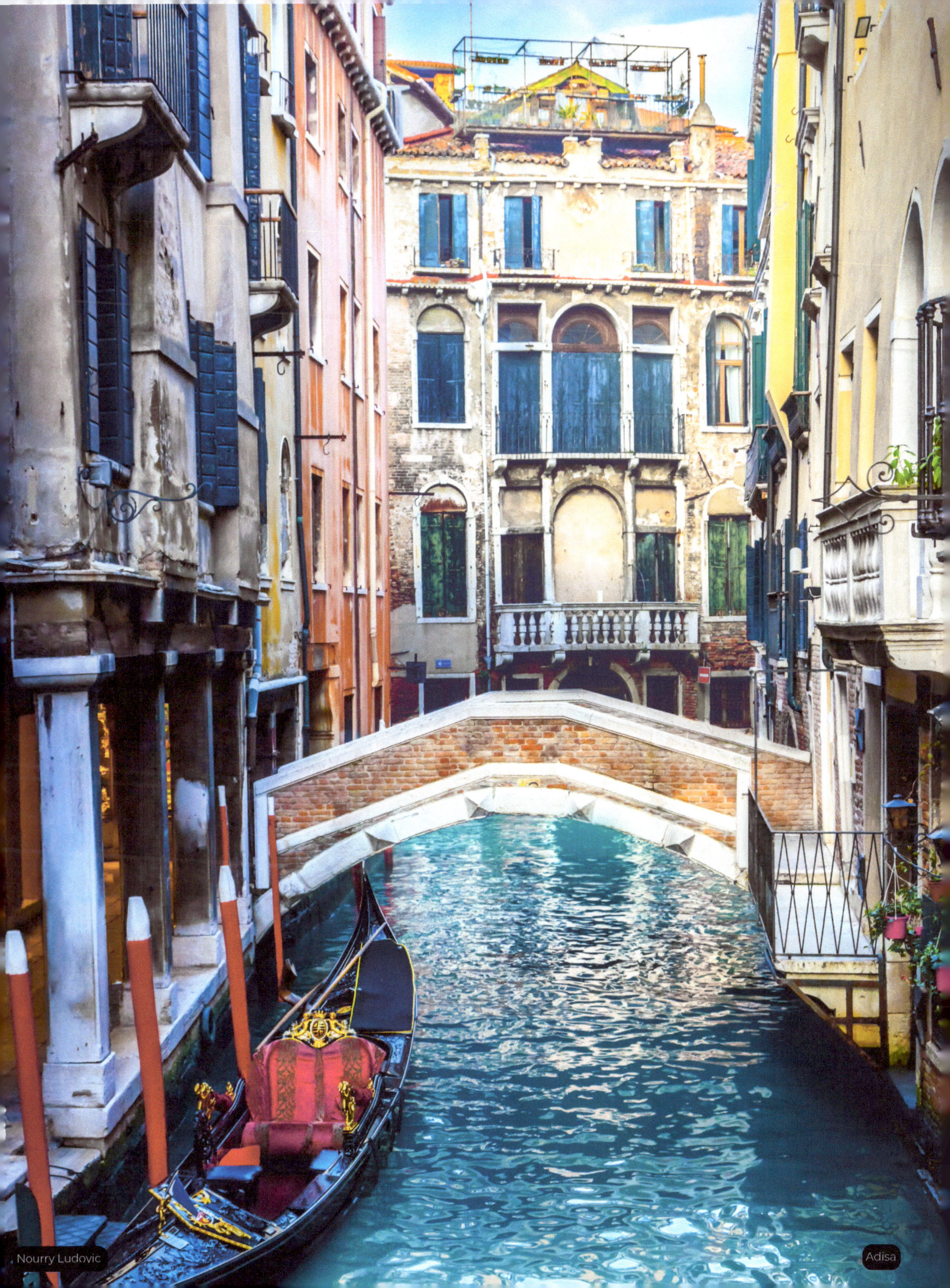

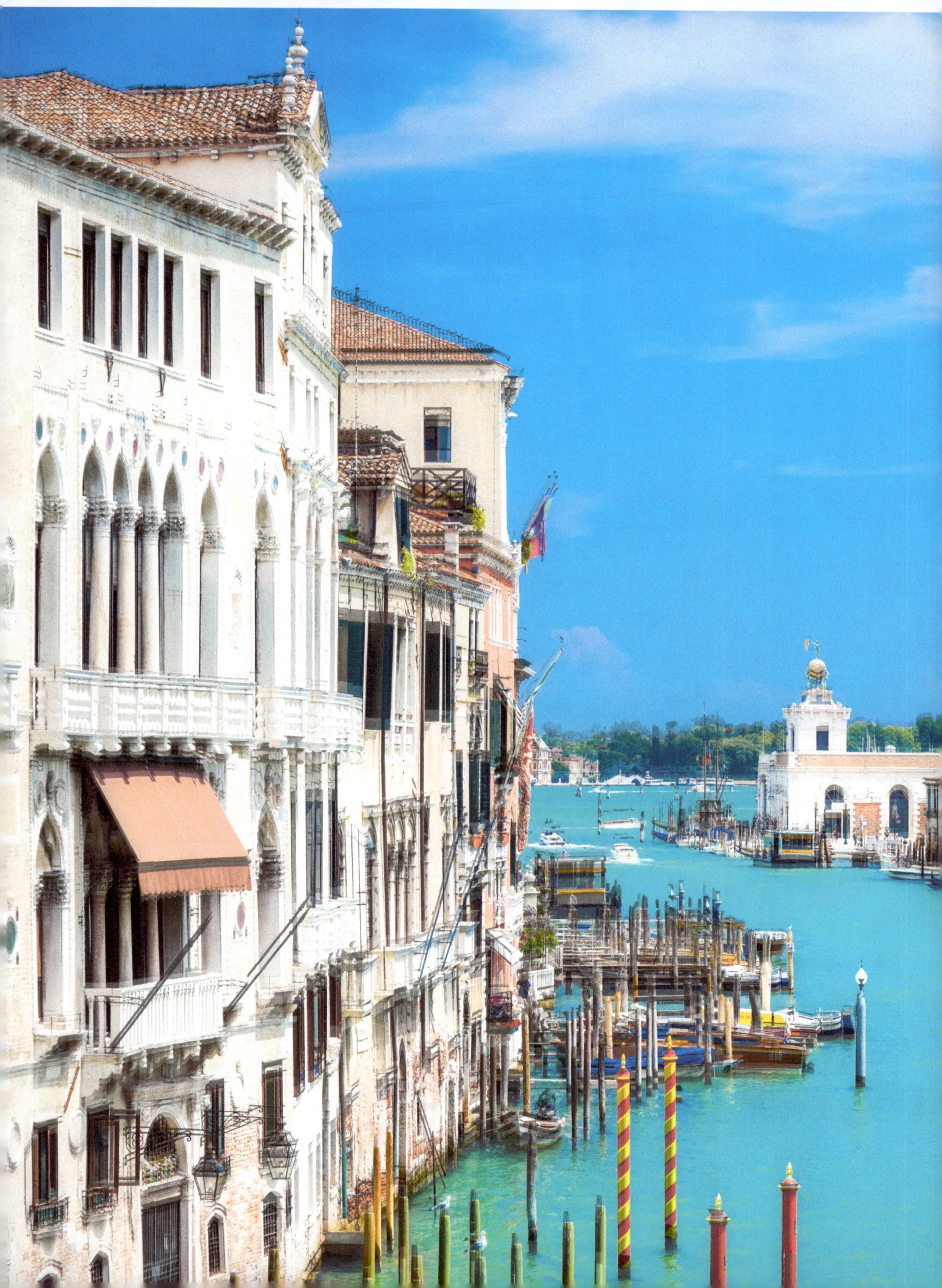

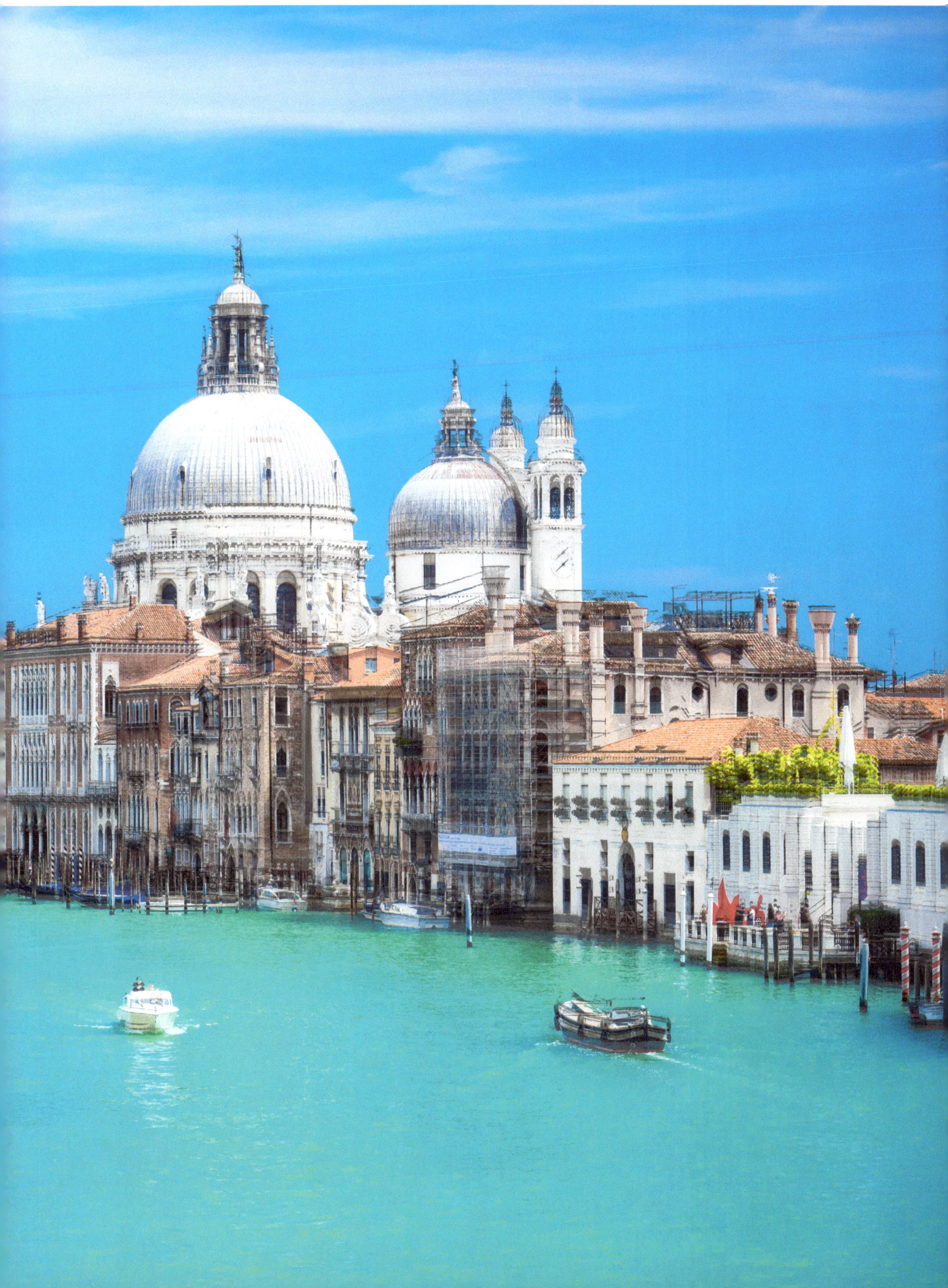

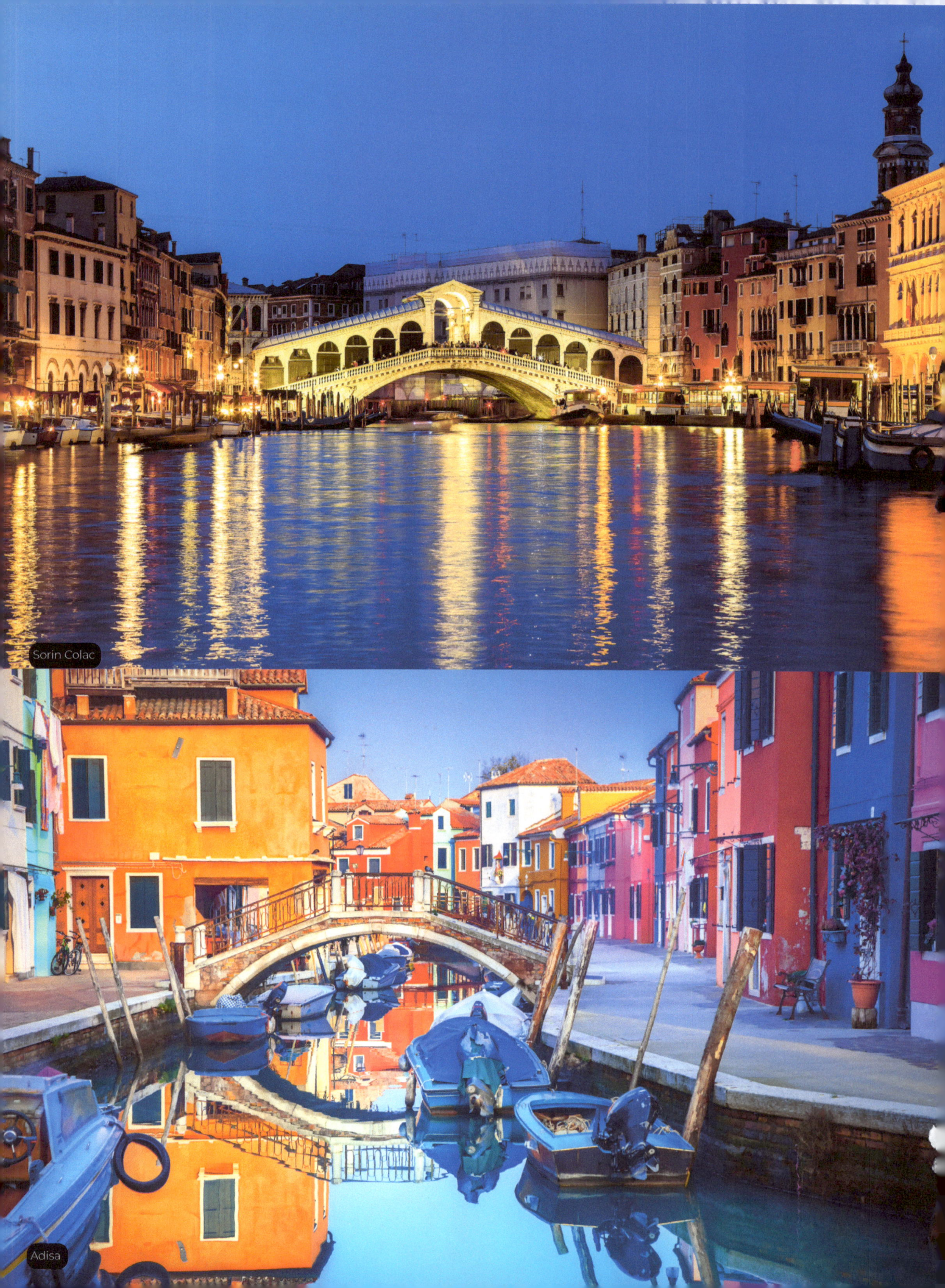

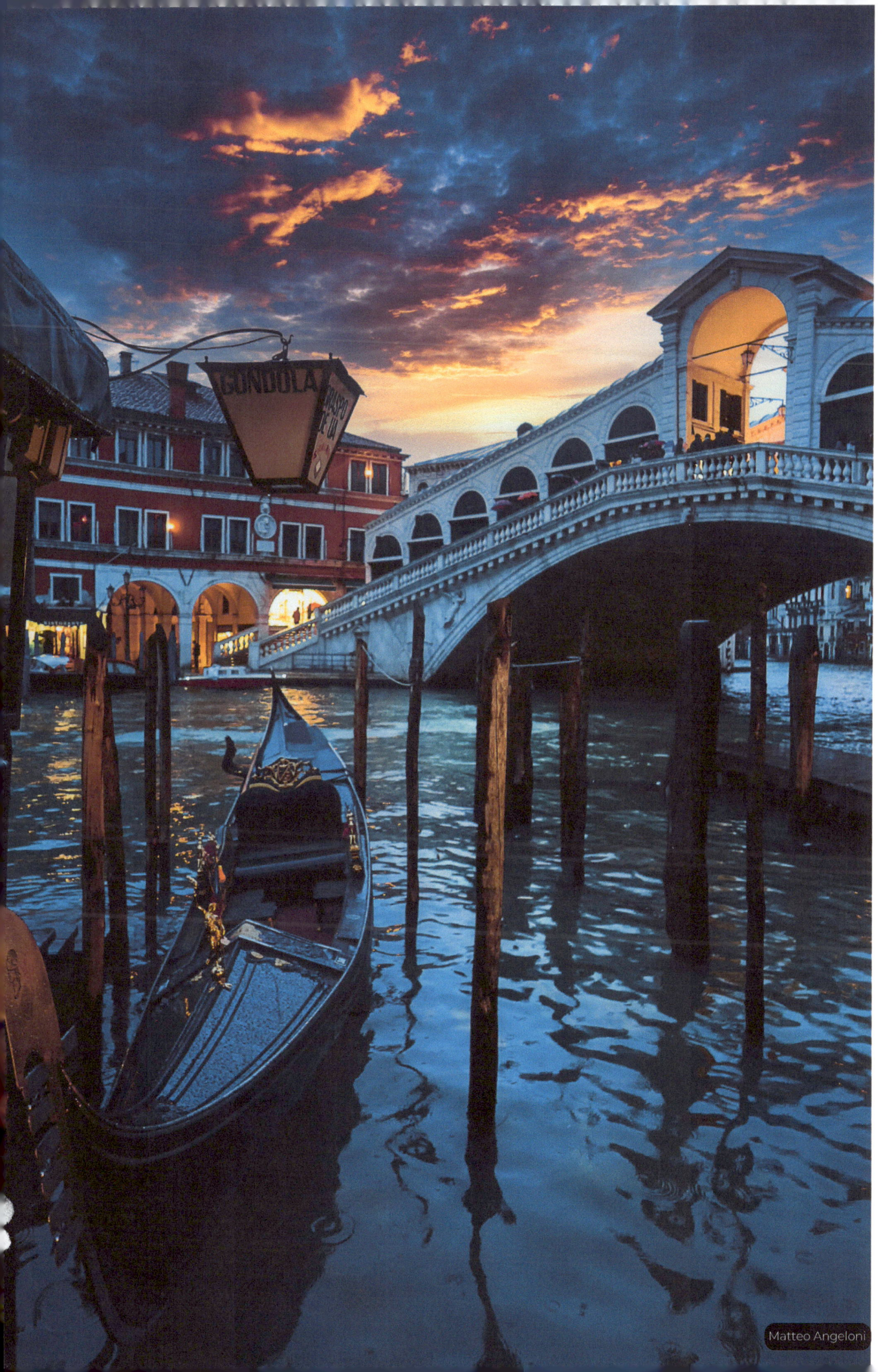

Torre Dell'Orologio

In the bustling Piazza San Marco, the Torre Dell'Orologio stands as a grand testament to Venice's ingenuity and artistic heritage. Erected in the late 15th century, this towering structure is more than just a clock tower; it's a symbol of the city's intricate relationship with time and the sea.

The clock's face, a splendid example of Renaissance artistry, features a mesmerizing blue and gold design. It not only displays the time but also the phases of the moon and the zodiac, a tribute to Venice's seafaring traditions and its reliance on celestial navigation. At the summit, two bronze figures, known as the "Moors," striking the bell on the hour add a sense of life and motion, marking the passage of time in a city seemingly suspended between past and present.

One of the tower's most enchanting features is its celebration of Venice's patron, St. Mark. Each Ascension Day, a mechanical parade of figures, led by an angel and the Magi, emerges to pay homage to a statue of the saint, capturing the city's enduring reverence for its protector.

The Torre Dell'Orologio is not merely a timepiece; it's a canvas that narrates Venice's rich history, astronomical knowledge, and artistic prowess, inviting travelers to delve deeper into the enchanting story of La Serenissima.

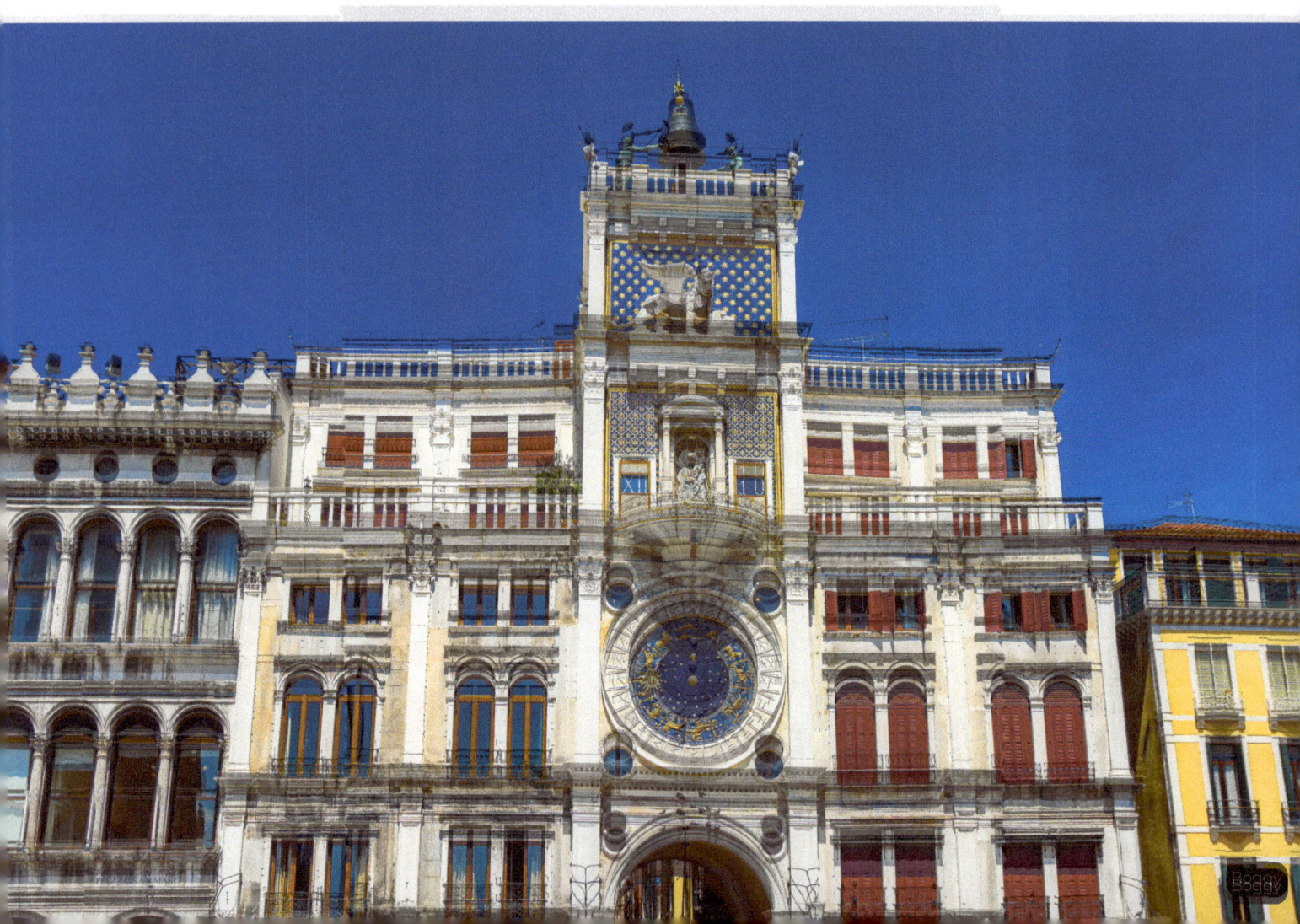

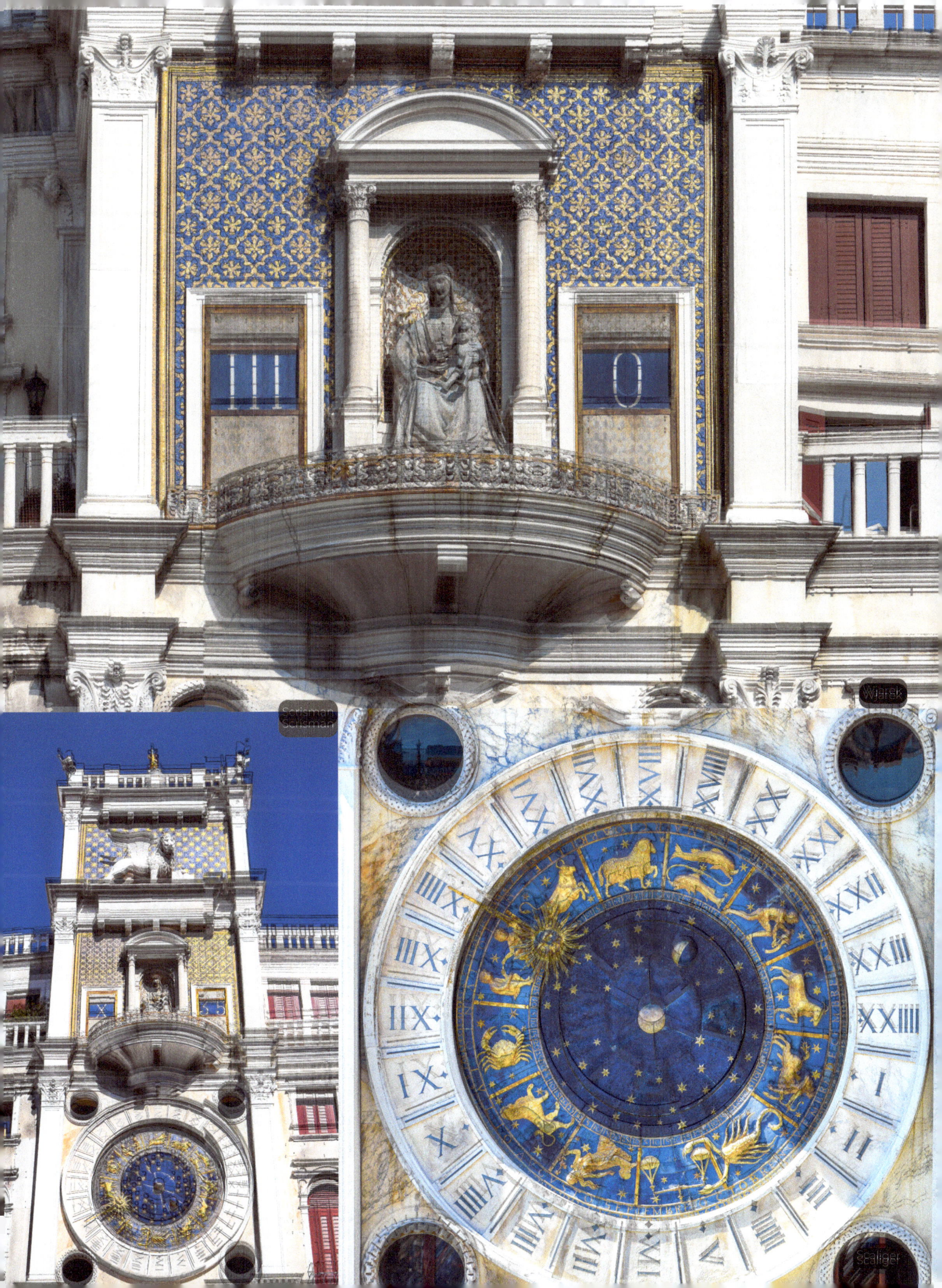

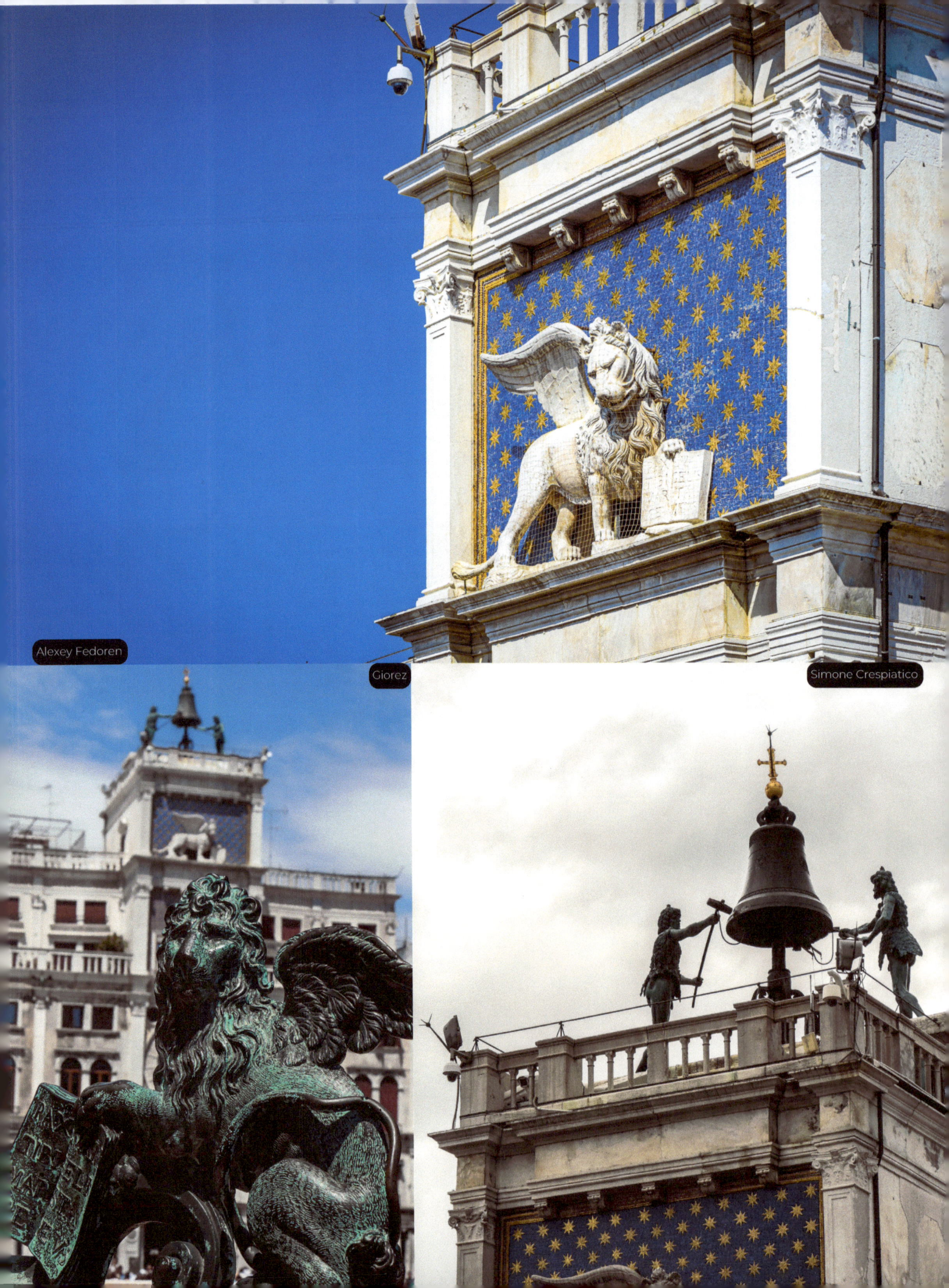

Alexey Fedoren

Giorez

Simone Crespiatico

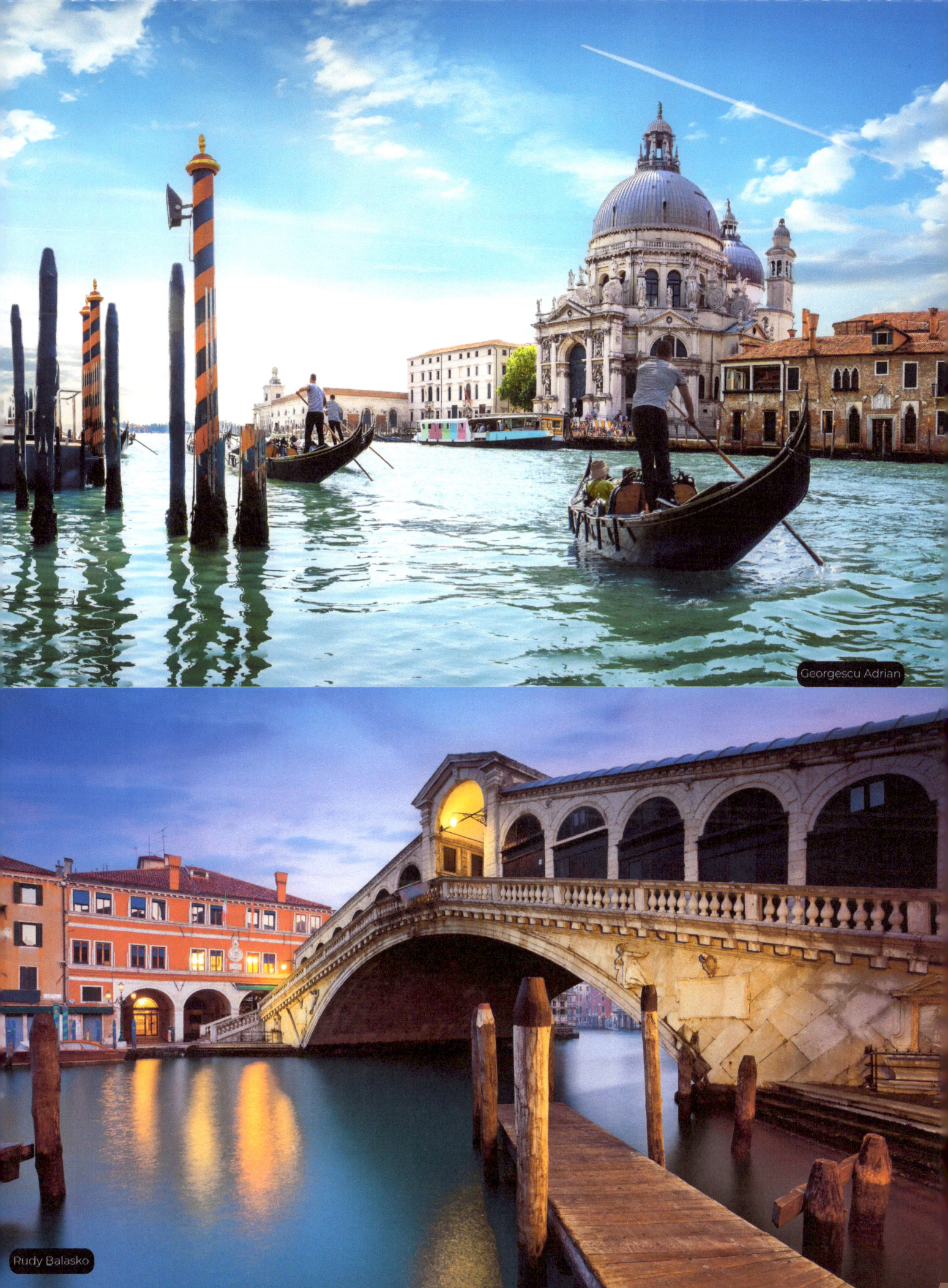

Palazzo Ducale

Overlooking the lagoon on the edge of Piazza San Marco, Palazzo Ducale stands as a stunning symbol of Venice's historical grandeur and political prowess. Originally built in the 9th century, it was the residence of the Doge and the heart of Venetian governance, embodying the city's wealth and power.

The Palazzo's exterior, a harmonious blend of Gothic and Renaissance elements, boasts a façade of white limestone and pink marble, creating an enchanting play of color and light. The ornate Porta della Carta, the main entrance, serves as a magnificent introduction to the palace's splendor, adorned with intricate sculptures and the Lion of St. Mark, symbolizing Venice's dominance.

Inside, the Palazzo Ducale unfolds like a treasure trove of art and history. The grandiose Scala d'Oro, an ornate golden staircase, leads to lavishly decorated chambers, each telling stories of Venice's past. The Sala del Maggior Consiglio, the largest room in the palace, is adorned with Tintoretto's masterpiece, "Paradise," one of the world's largest oil paintings, illustrating the artistic zenith of the Venetian Republic.

Exploring the Palazzo Ducale is not just a journey through a building, but a voyage into the heart of Venice's legacy – a blend of governance, art, and the unique spirit of a city that reigned over the seas.

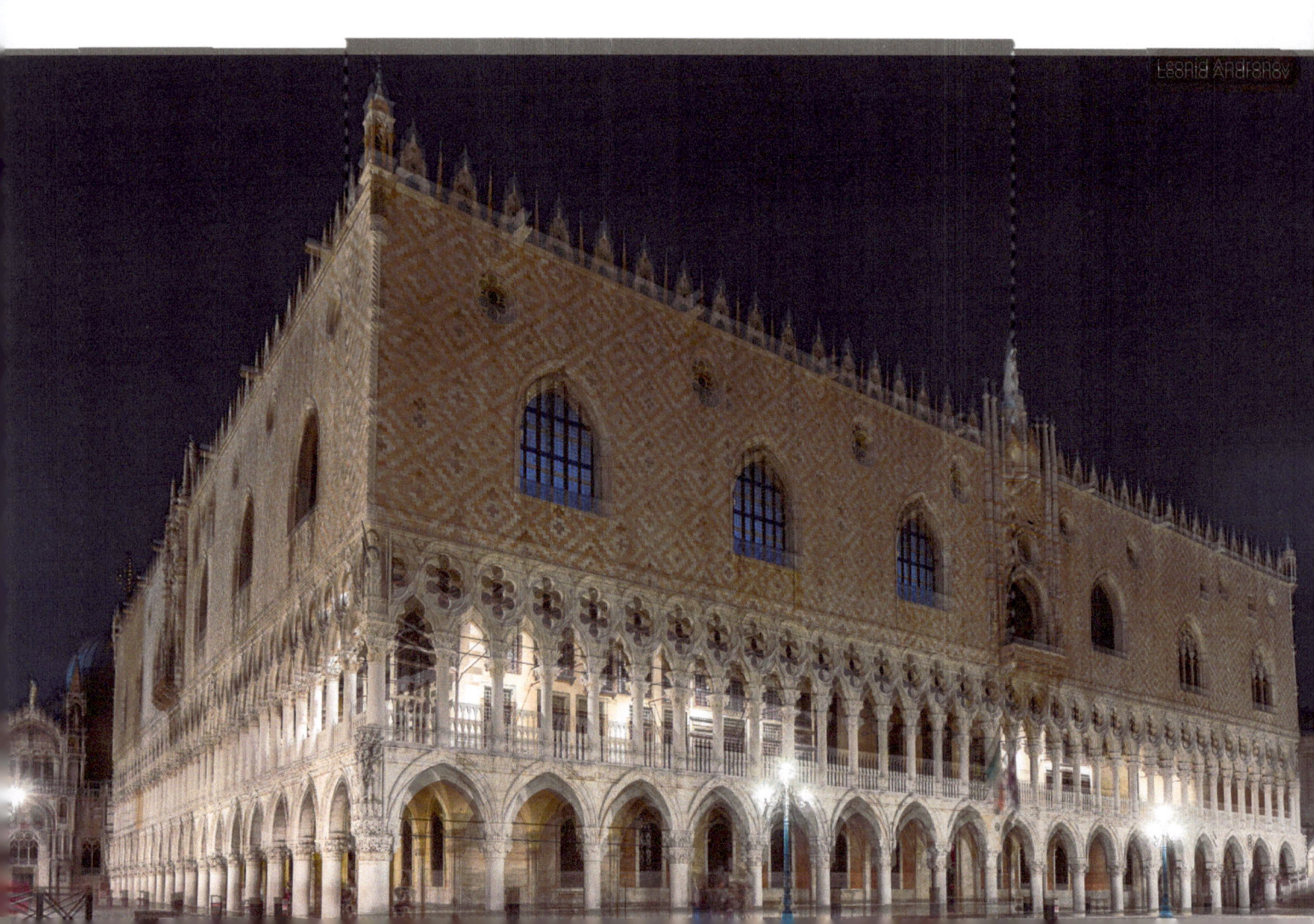

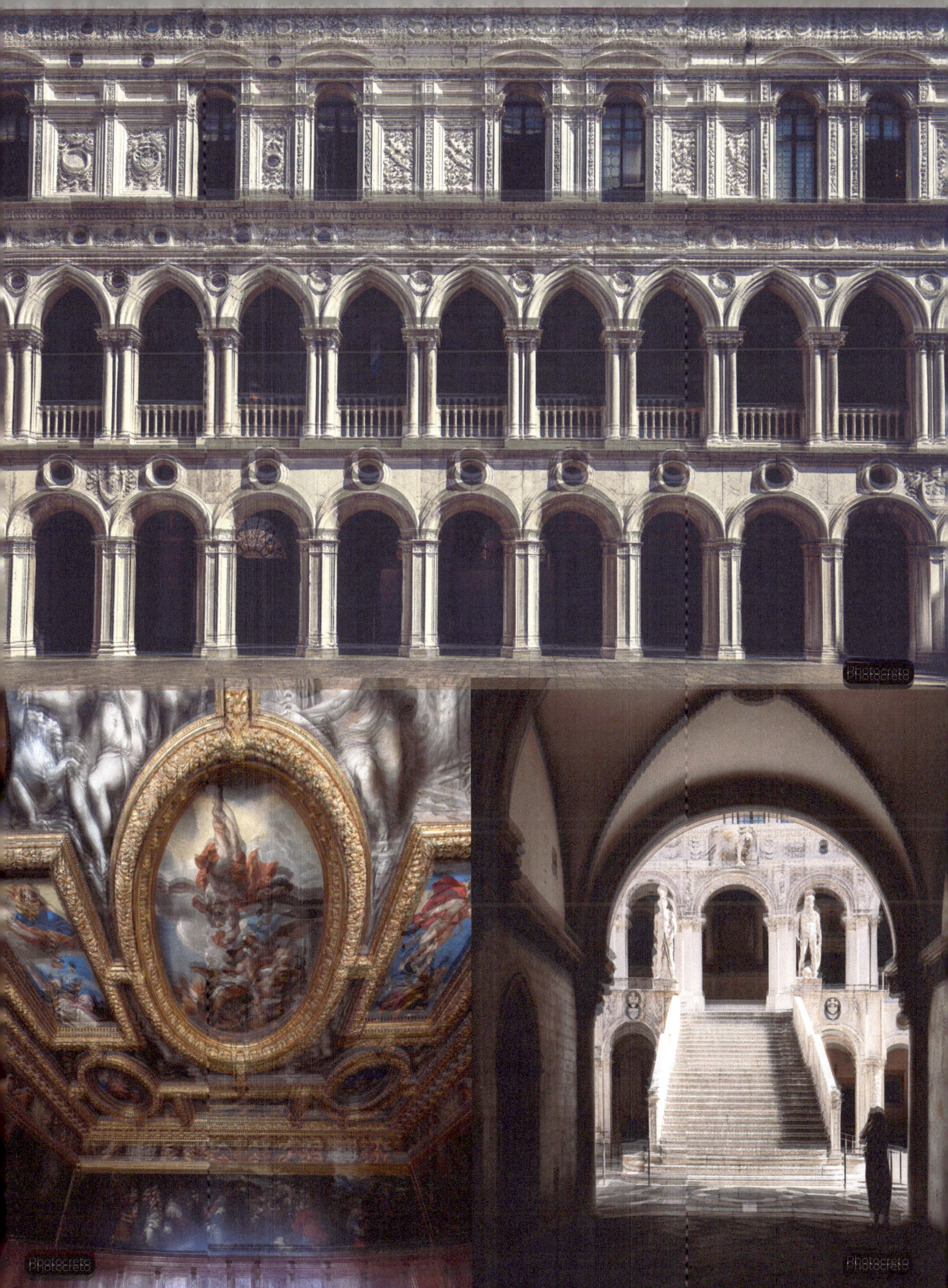

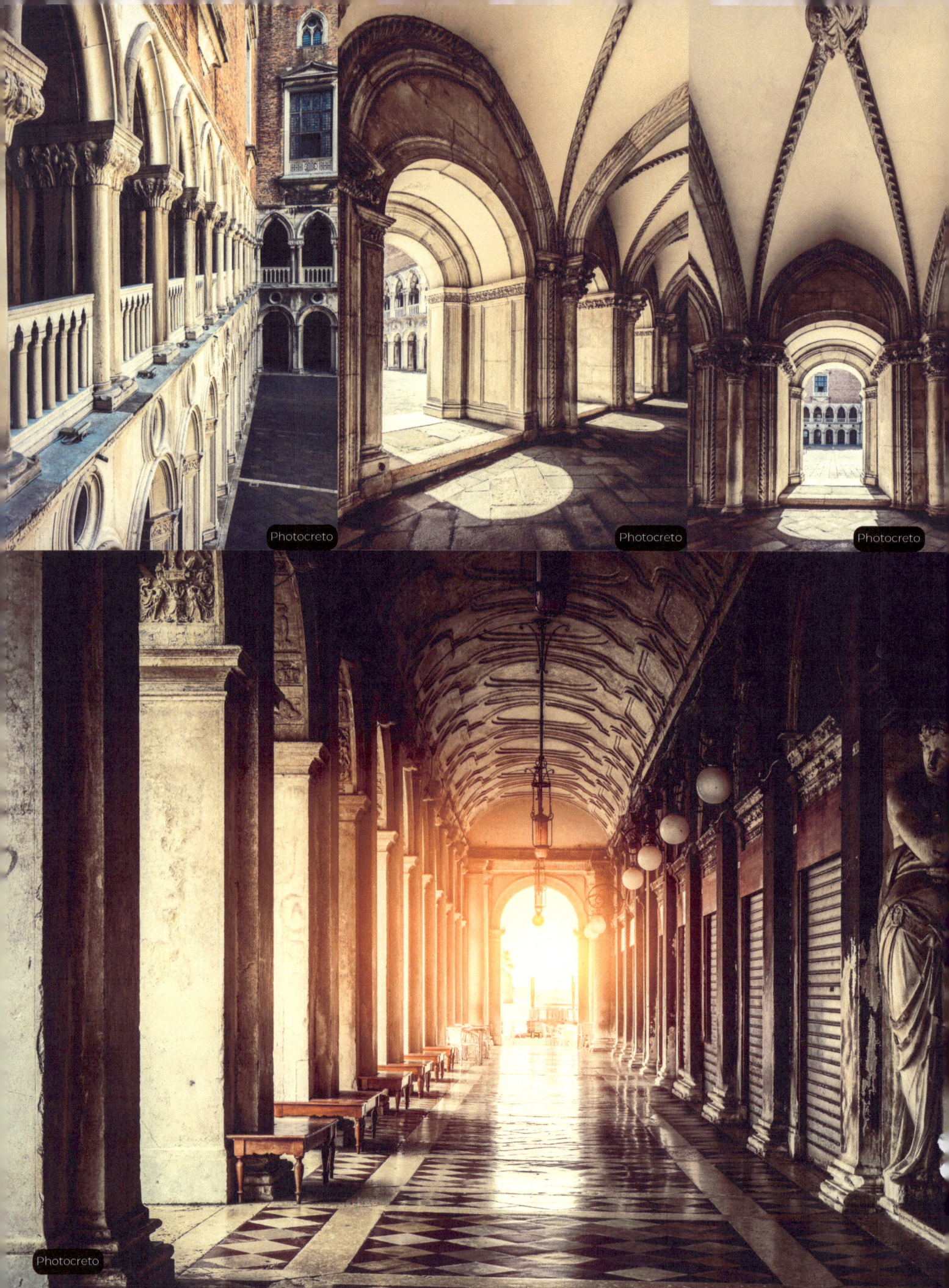

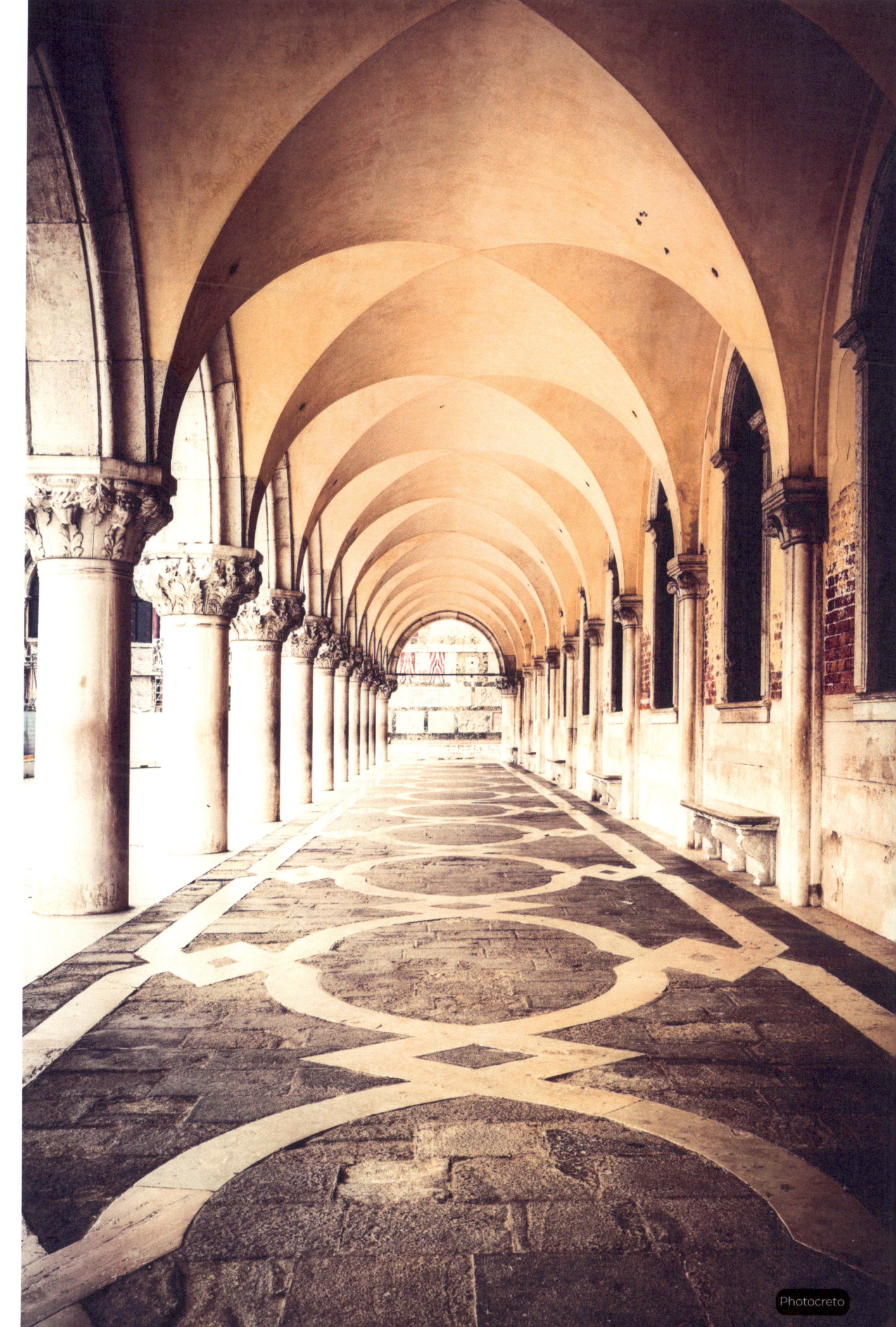

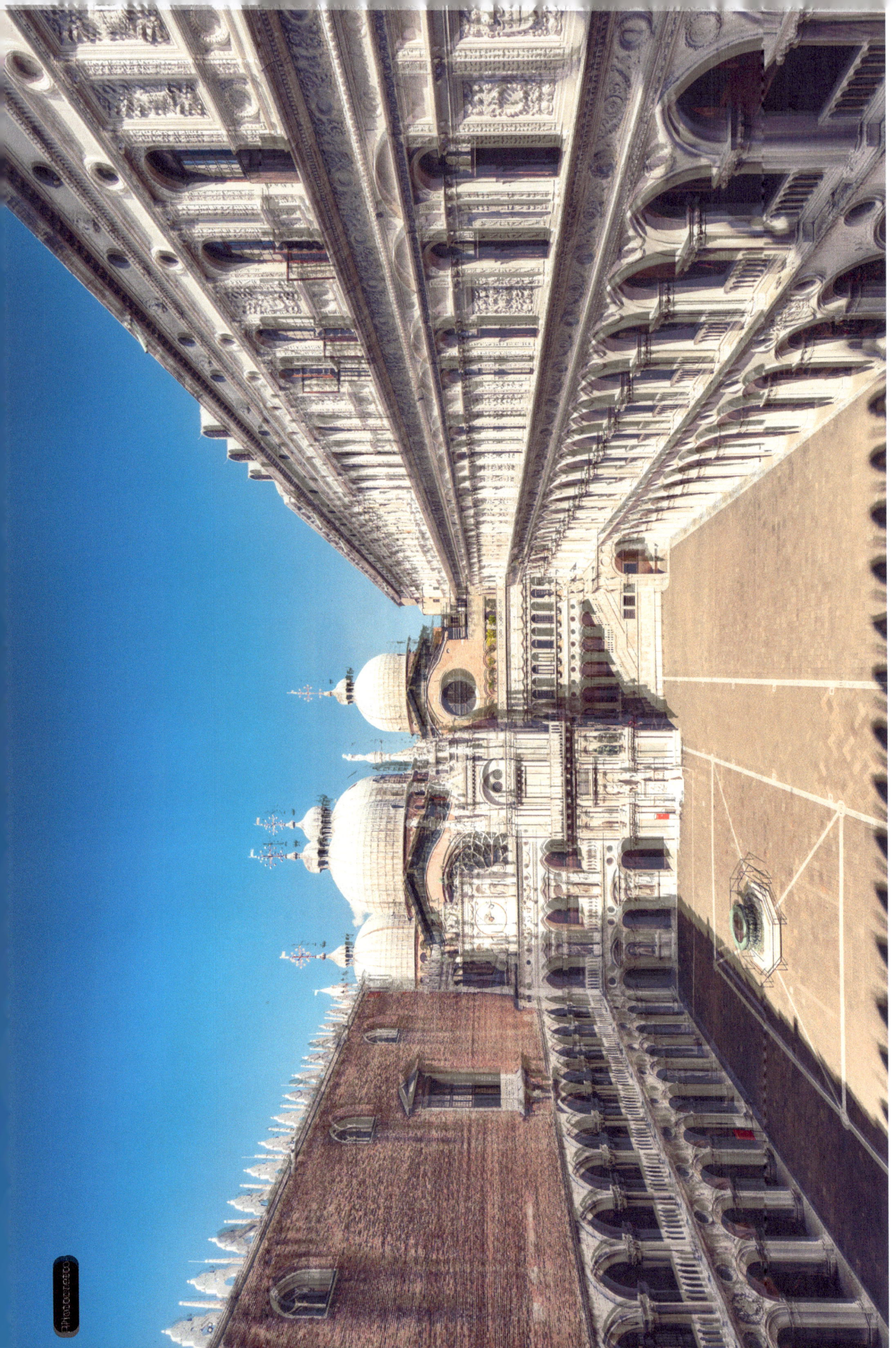

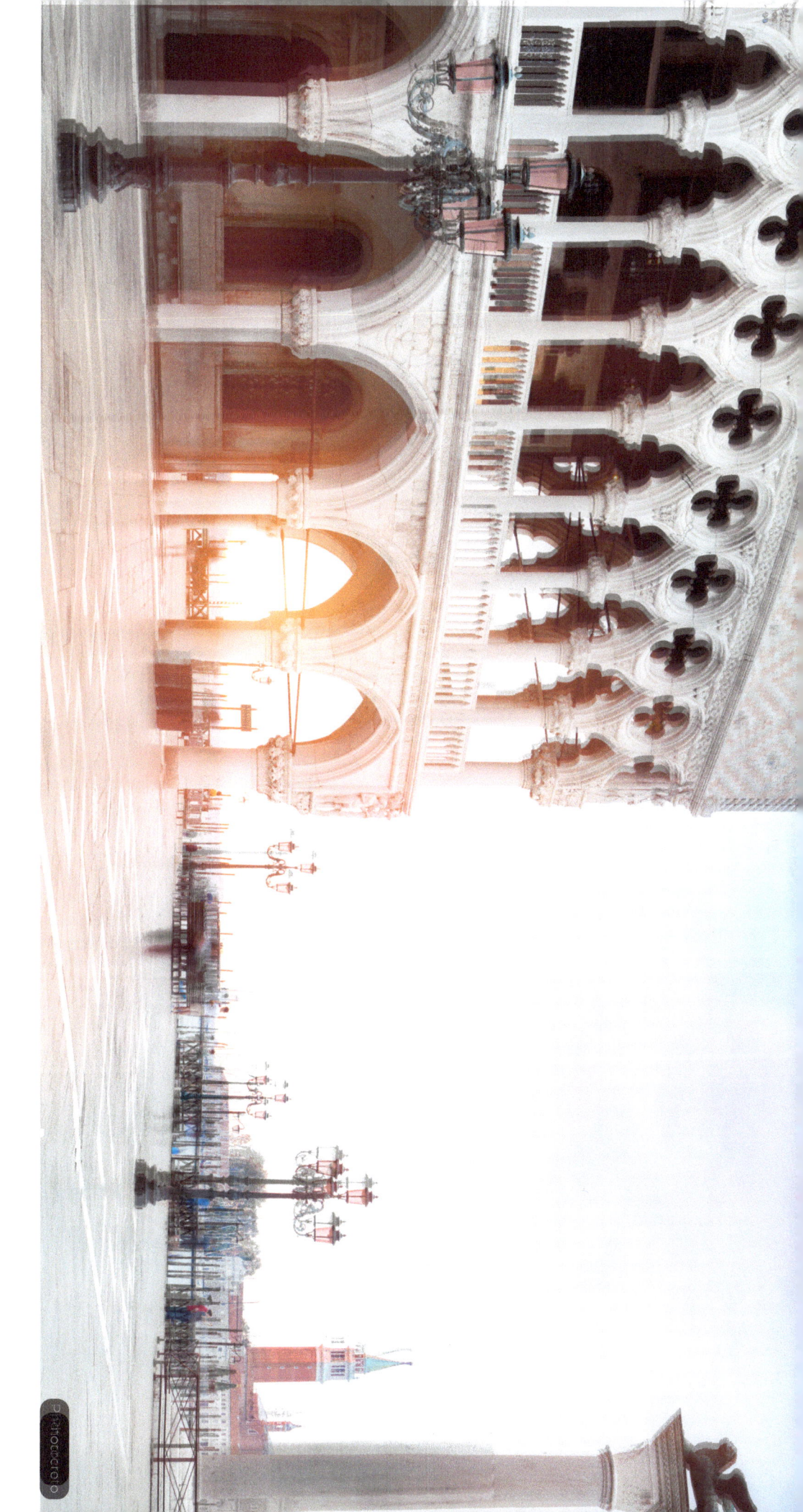

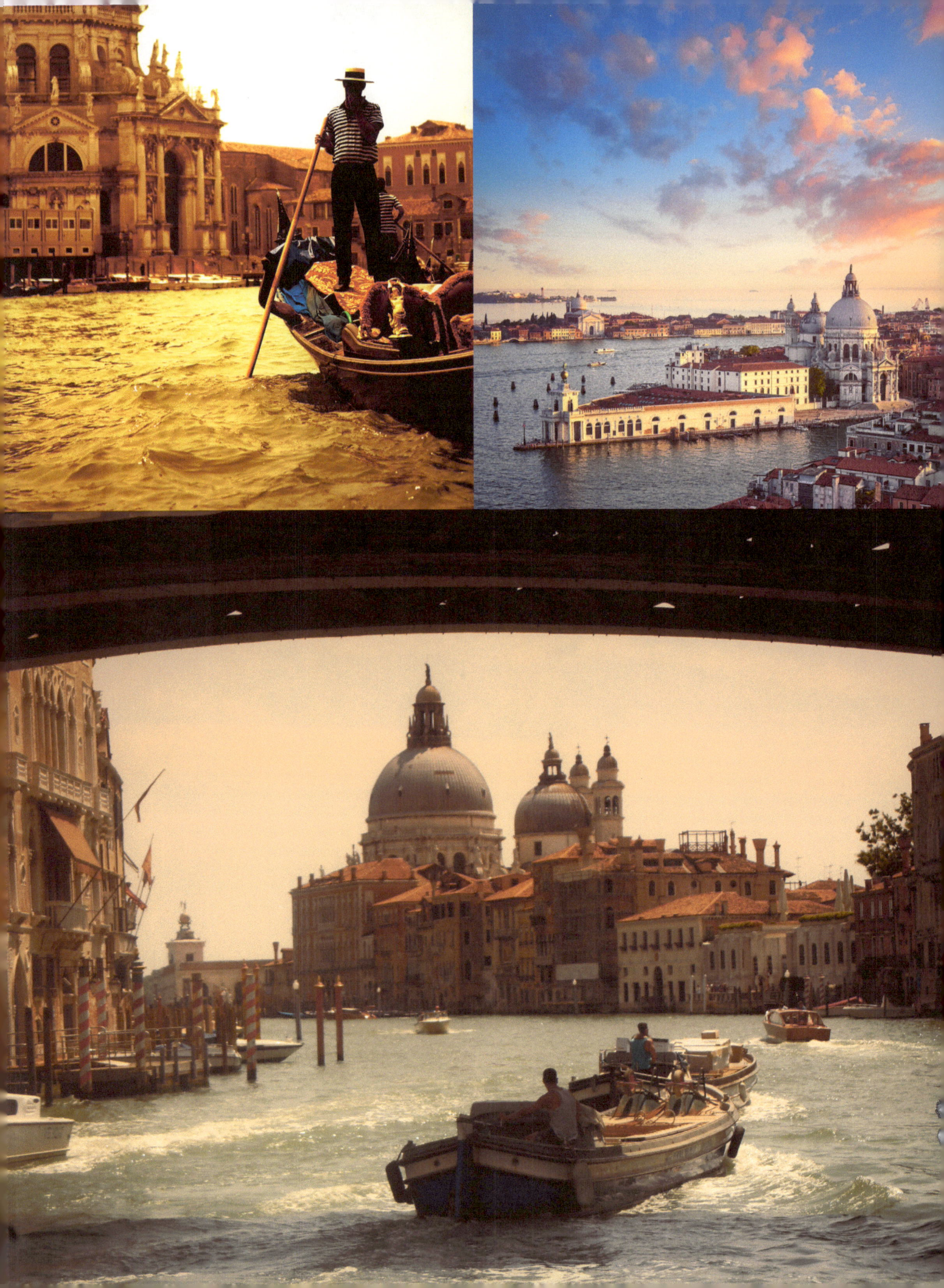

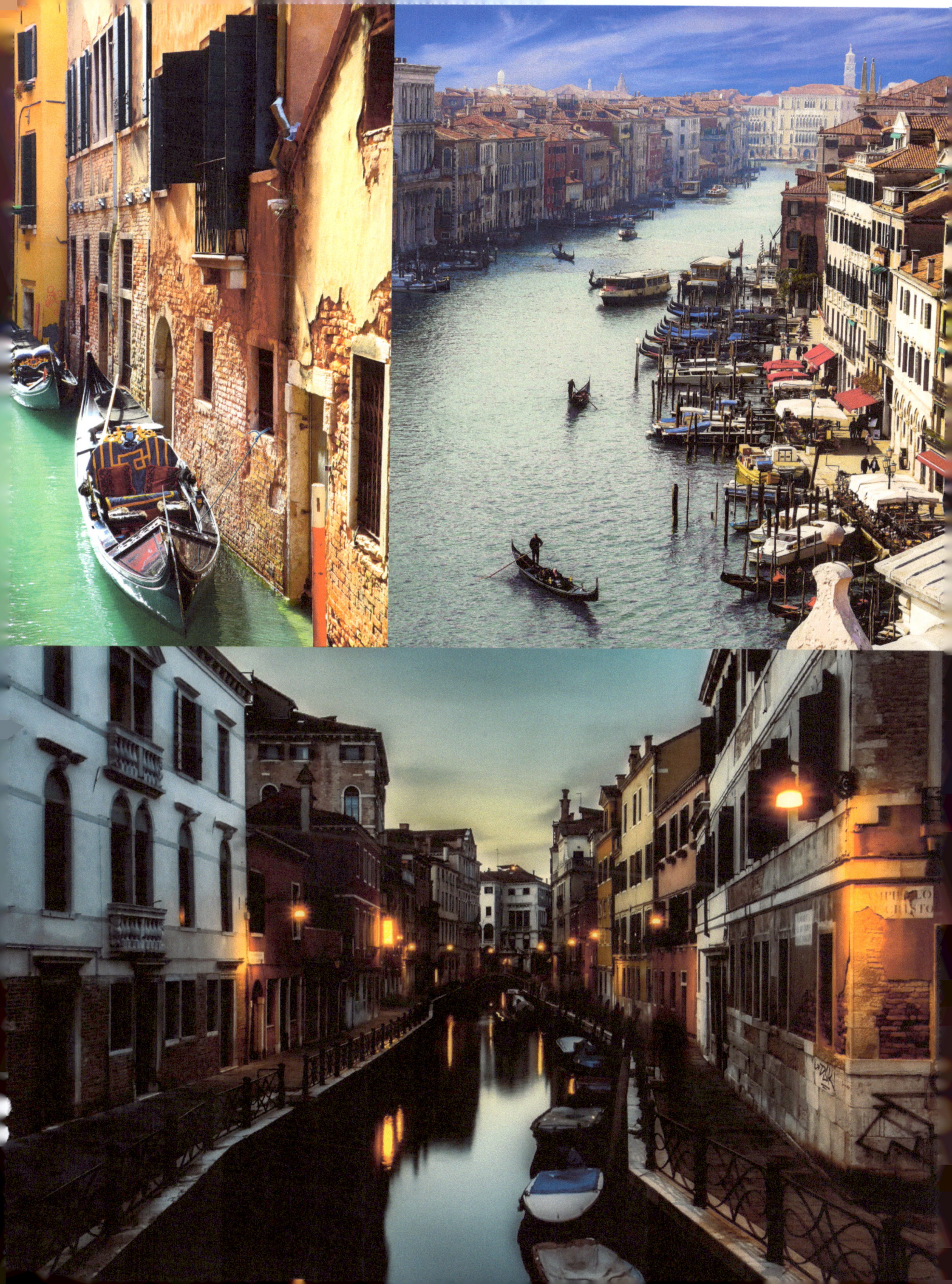

Campanile di San Marco

Rising majestically in Piazza San Marco, the Campanile di San Marco is not just Venice's tallest structure but also an iconic symbol of the city's historical and architectural grandeur. Originally built in the 9th century and reconstructed in 1912 after a collapse, this bell tower offers a tangible connection to Venice's storied past.

The Campanile's simple, yet elegant form, standing at 98.6 meters, dominates the Venetian skyline. Its red brick facade, capped with a pyramidal spire and a golden weathervane in the form of the Archangel Gabriel, reflects the blend of Byzantine and Renaissance influences that characterize Venetian architecture.

Visitors venturing to the top are rewarded with a breathtaking panorama of Venice's rooftops, winding canals, and distant islands, a view that encapsulates the beauty and uniqueness of the city. The sight of the lagoon stretching infinitely, interspersed with the delicate silhouettes of gondolas and vaporettos, is a moment of pure, awe-inspiring beauty.

The Campanile di San Marco is more than a landmark; it is a sentinel watching over centuries of Venetian history. Its presence in the city's heart invites travelers to gaze out and contemplate the timeless allure of Venice, a city that floats serenely between the sea and the sky.

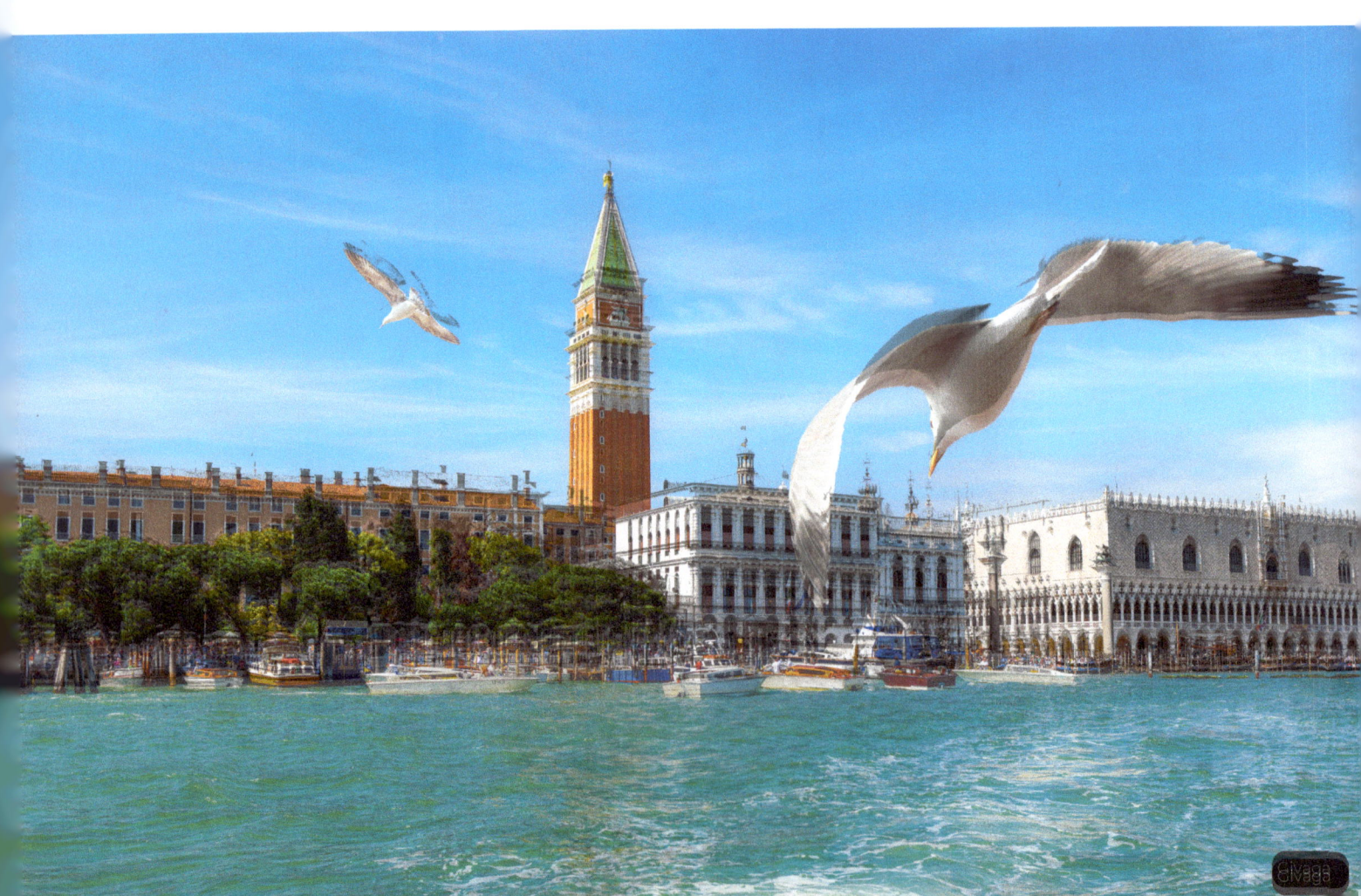

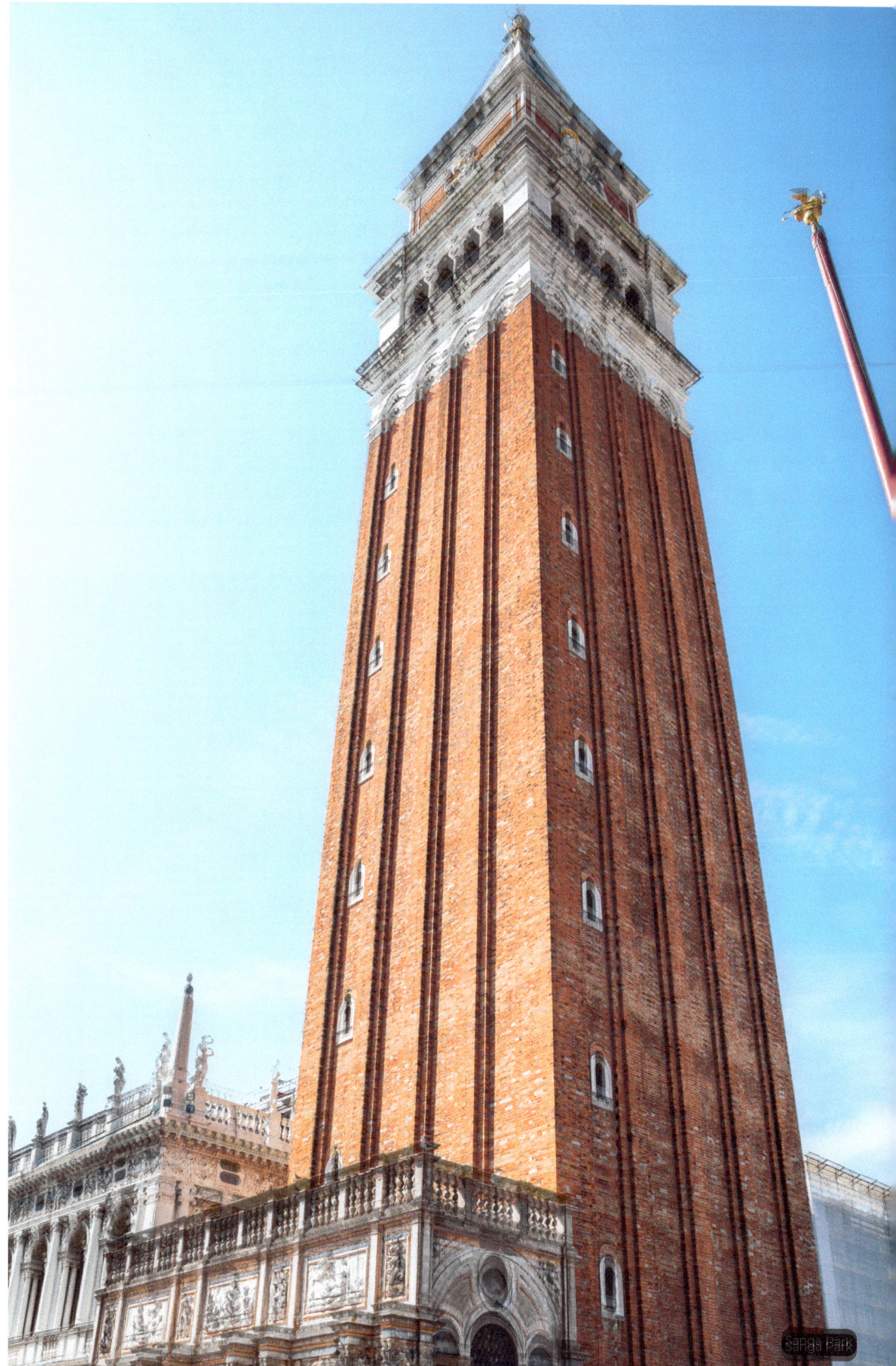

Ca' d'Oro

On the banks of the Grand Canal, the Ca' d'Oro (Golden House) stands as a breathtaking example of Venetian Gothic architecture. Built in the mid-15th century for the Contarini family, one of Venice's most prominent families, this palazzo exemplifies the opulence and artistry of its era.

Originally adorned with gold leaf, polychrome, and ultramarine, the Ca' d'Oro's façade once shimmered in the sunlight, reflecting off the canal's waters. Although much of the gold has since faded, the building's intricate design, characterized by elegant, lace-like stone filigree, remains a testament to the wealth and sophistication of its creators.

Today, the Ca' d'Oro houses the Galleria Giorgio Franchetti, a museum boasting a rich collection of Venetian art. The artworks, including masterpieces by Titian, Mantegna, and Carpaccio, are displayed amidst the stunning backdrop of the palazzo's ornate interior, creating a harmonious blend of art and architecture.

Visitors to the Ca' d'Oro are transported into a world of Venetian grandeur, where every corner reveals a story of the city's past glories. Standing on its balcony overlooking the Grand Canal, one can't help but feel a connection to the generations of Venetians who witnessed the ebb and flow of life in this extraordinary city.

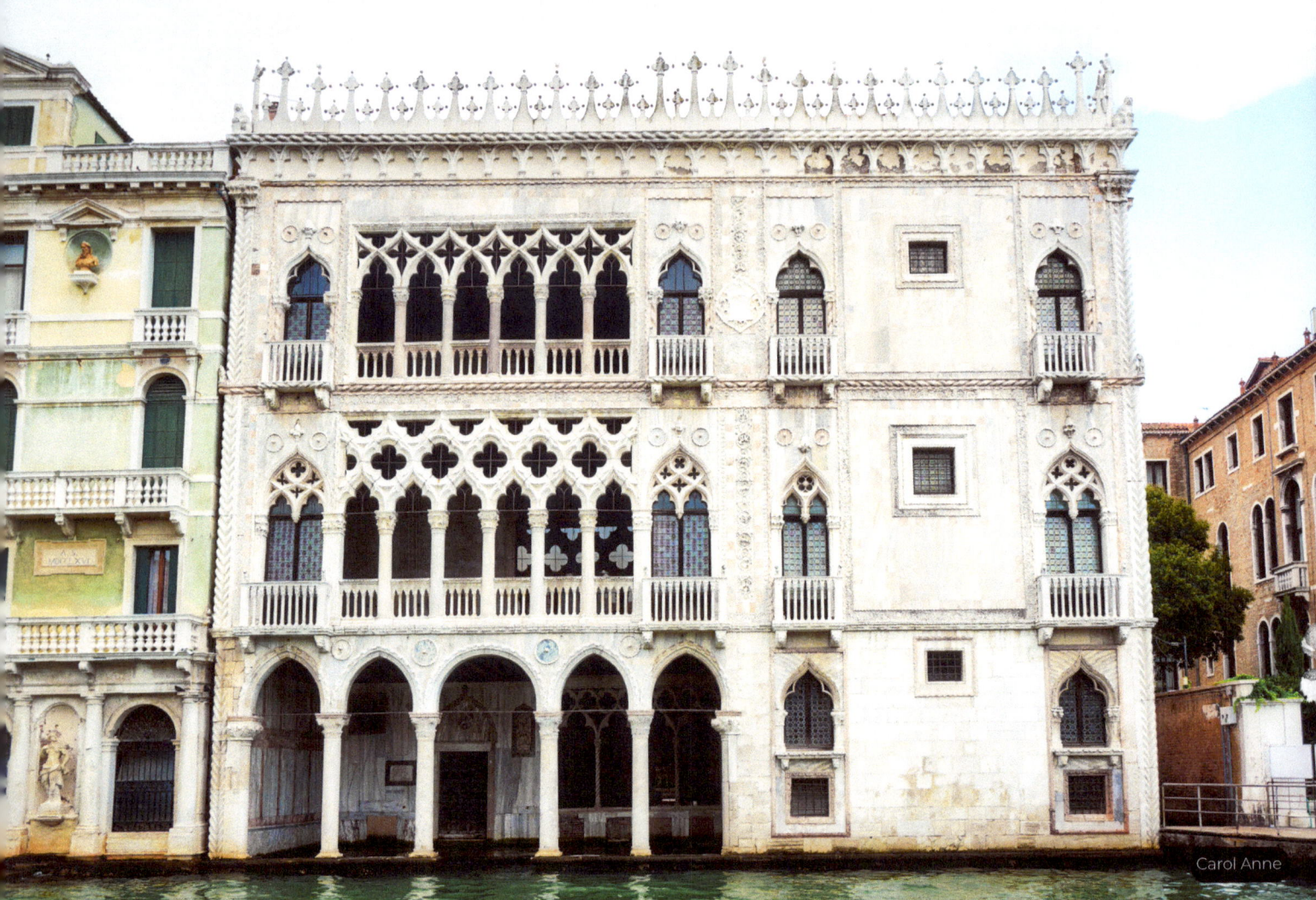

Carol Anne

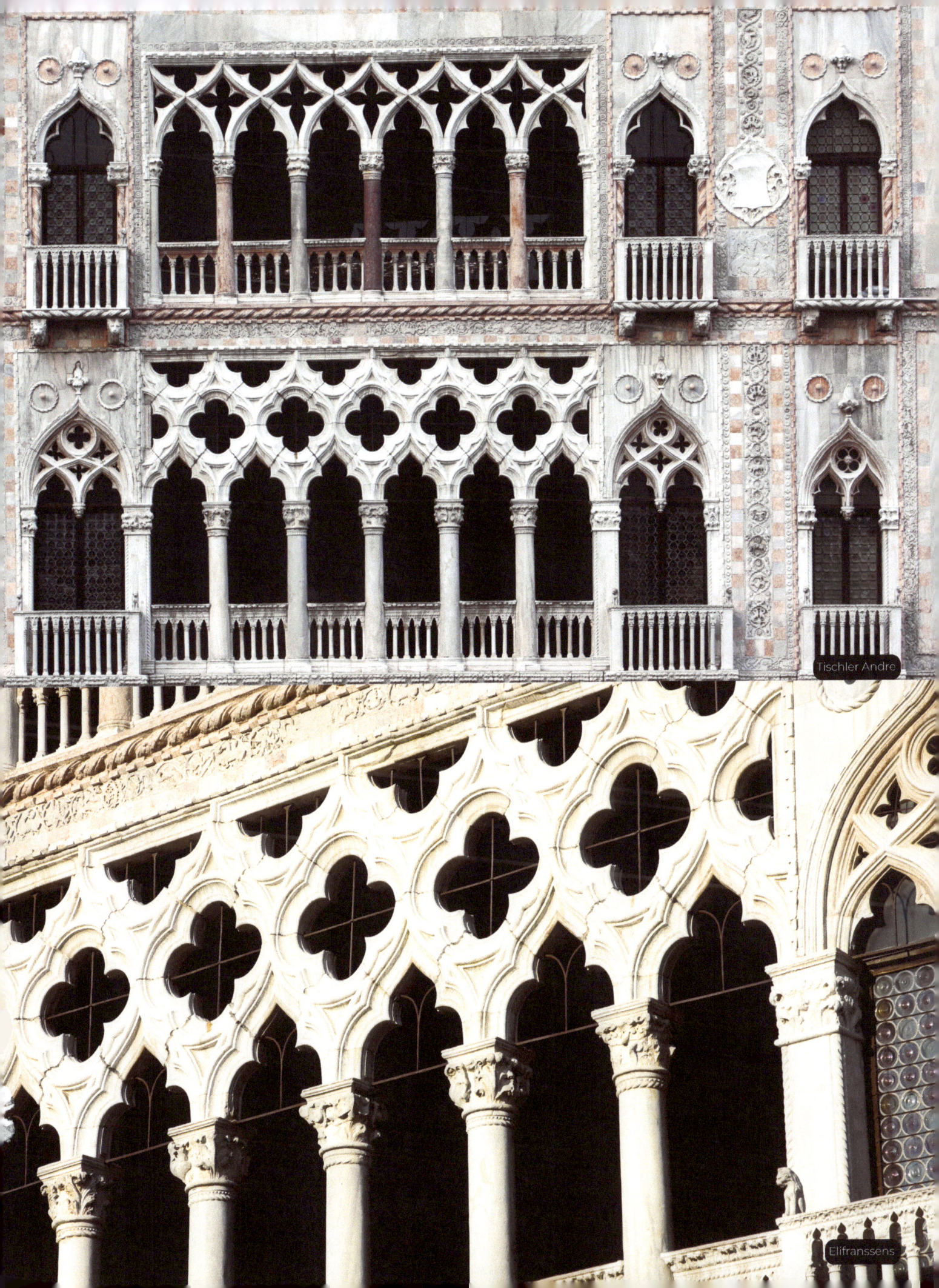

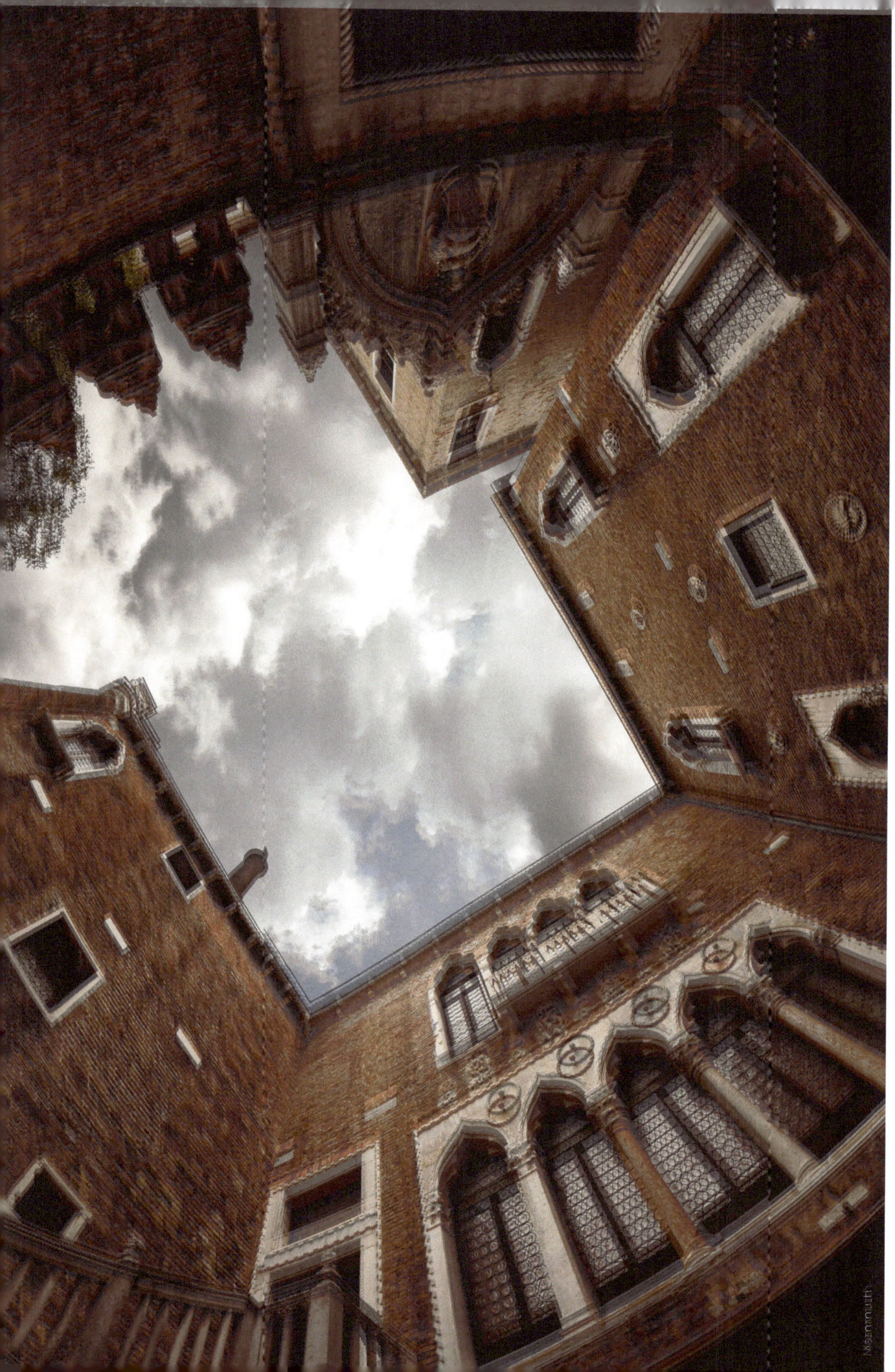

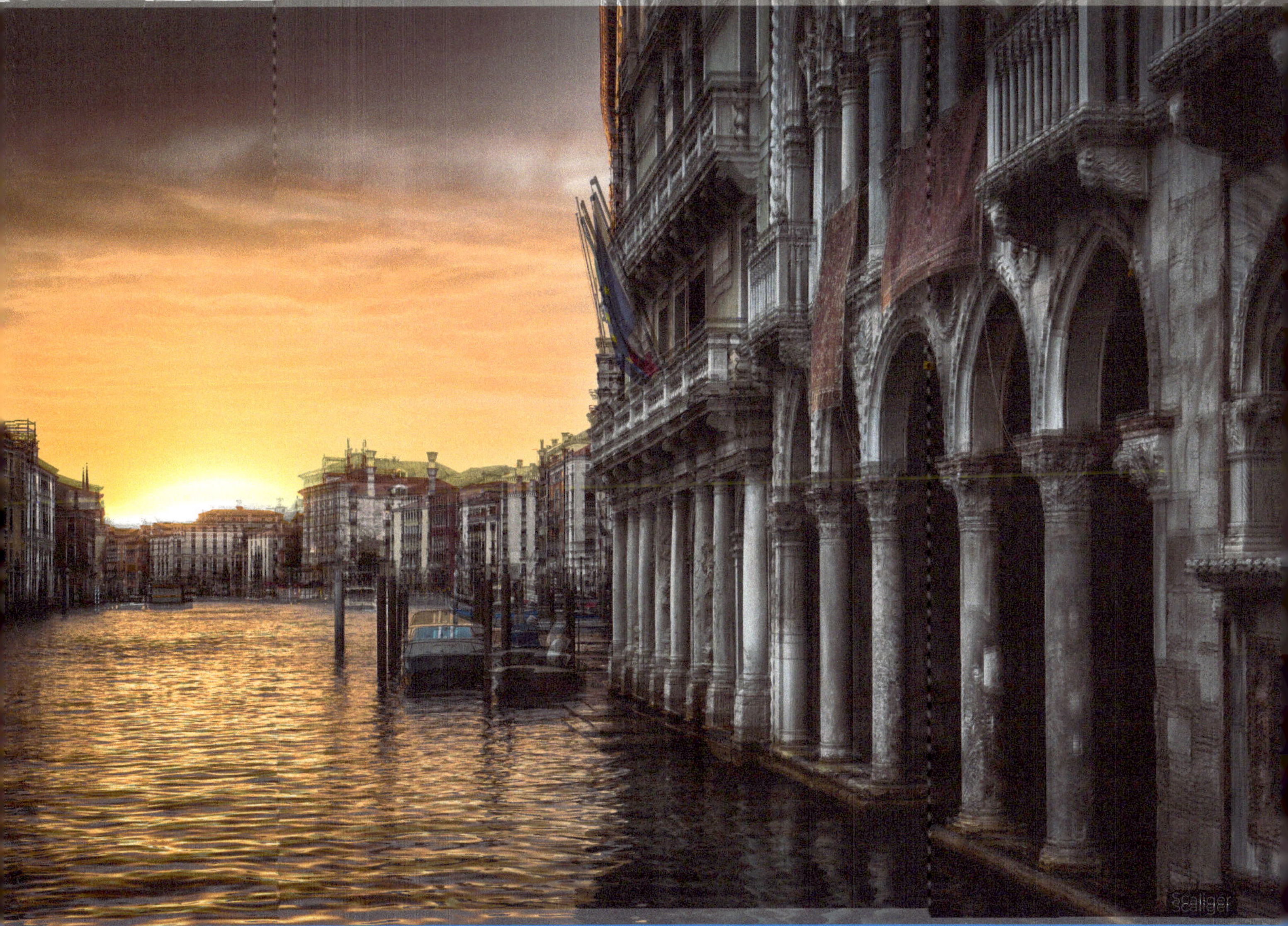

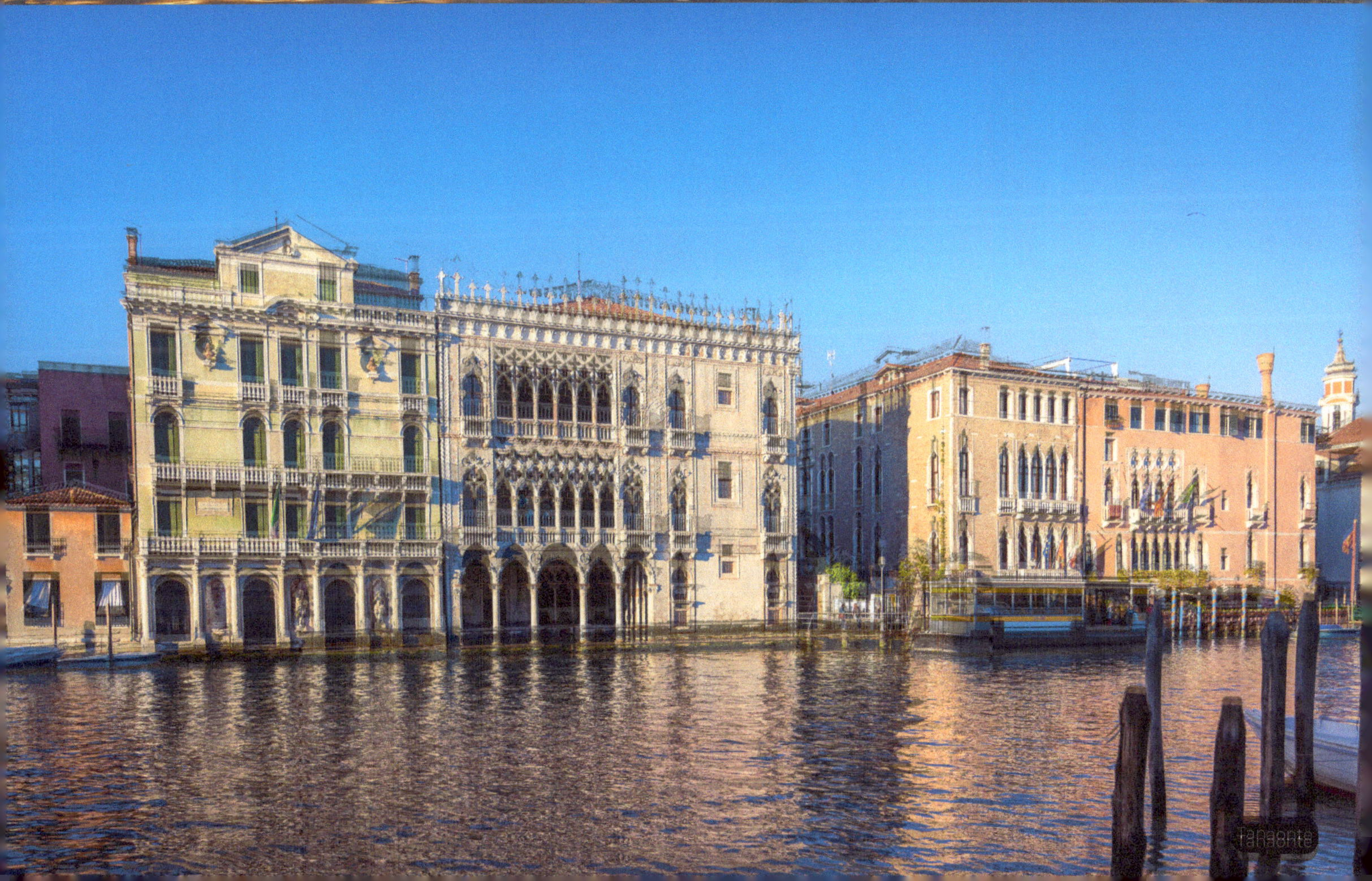

Santa Maria Assunta - I Gesuiti

In the Cannaregio district of Venice lies the Church of Santa Maria Assunta, known colloquially as I Gesuiti. This 18th-century Baroque masterpiece, with its rich history dating back to the 12th century, stands as a testament to Venice's enduring spiritual and artistic heritage.

The church's façade, an intricate tapestry of sculpted figures and ornamental motifs, captures the essence of Baroque artistry. It draws the eye upward, from the bustling street to the heavens, in a dynamic interplay of form and spirituality. The façade's grandeur is a prelude to the treasures housed within.

Stepping inside, visitors are enveloped in a realm of opulent beauty. The interior of I Gesuiti is a marvel of artistic craftsmanship. Its walls and ceilings are adorned with works by prominent Venetian artists, creating a visual symphony of biblical scenes and saintly figures. Notably, the church houses Titian's awe-inspiring "Martyrdom of St. Lawrence," a masterpiece that epitomizes the dramatic intensity of Venetian painting.

Perhaps the most striking feature is the illusion of sumptuous fabrics depicted in marble. This unique characteristic exemplifies the Venetian flair for blending art with illusion, leaving visitors mesmerized by the ingenuity and elegance on display.

Santa Maria Assunta - I Gesuiti is not just a church; it's a celebration of faith, art, and the transcendent beauty that defines Venice.

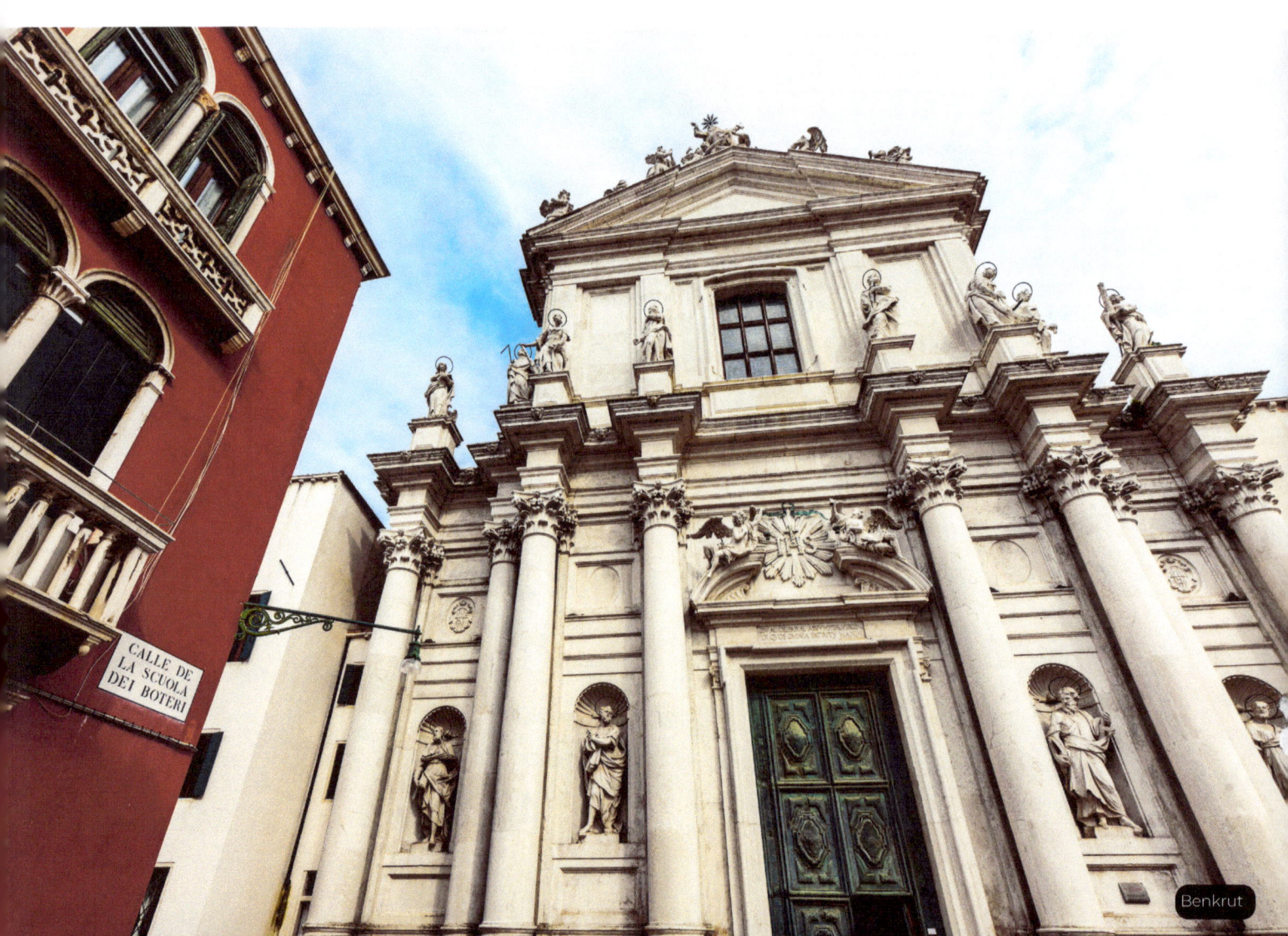

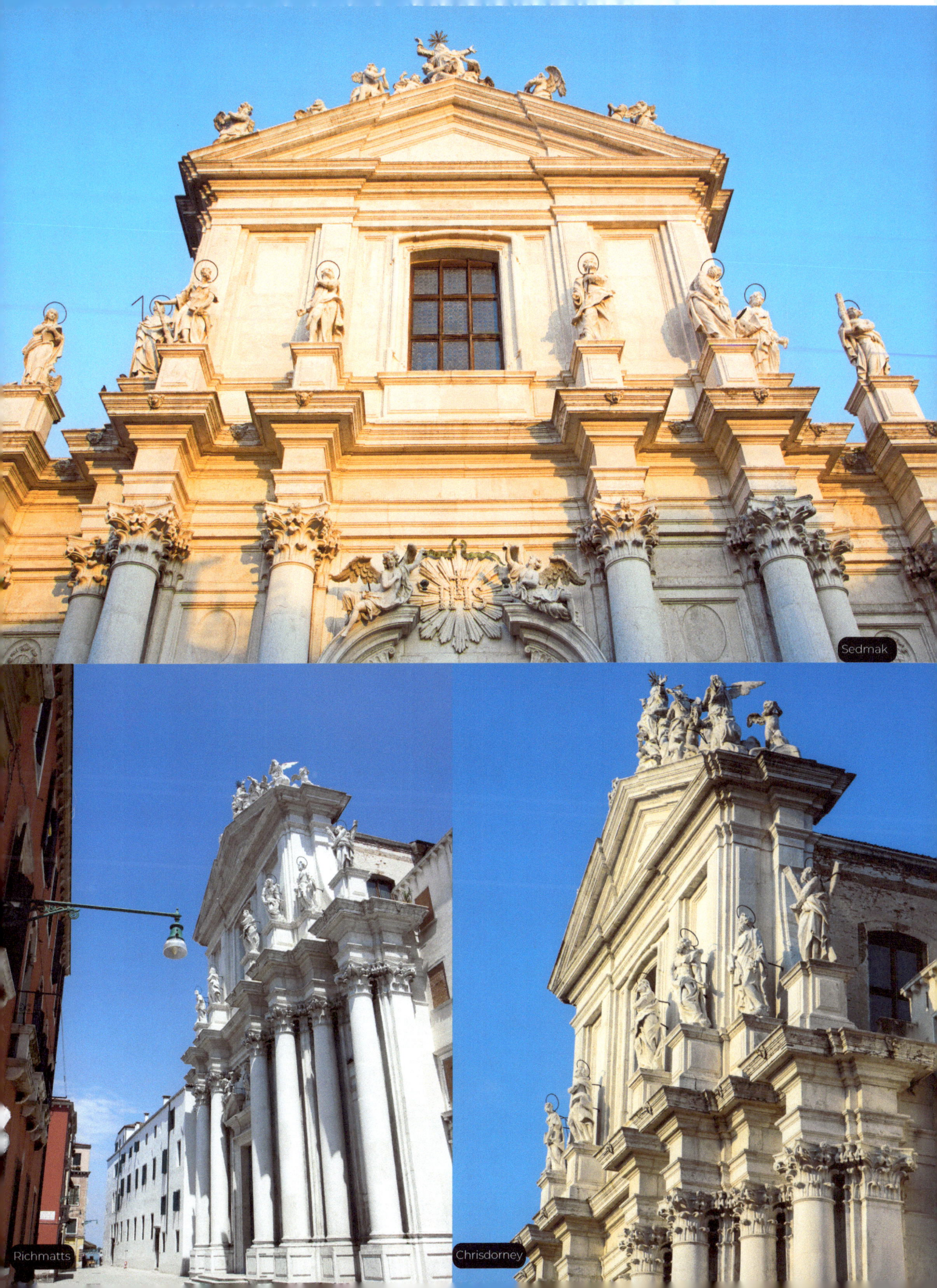

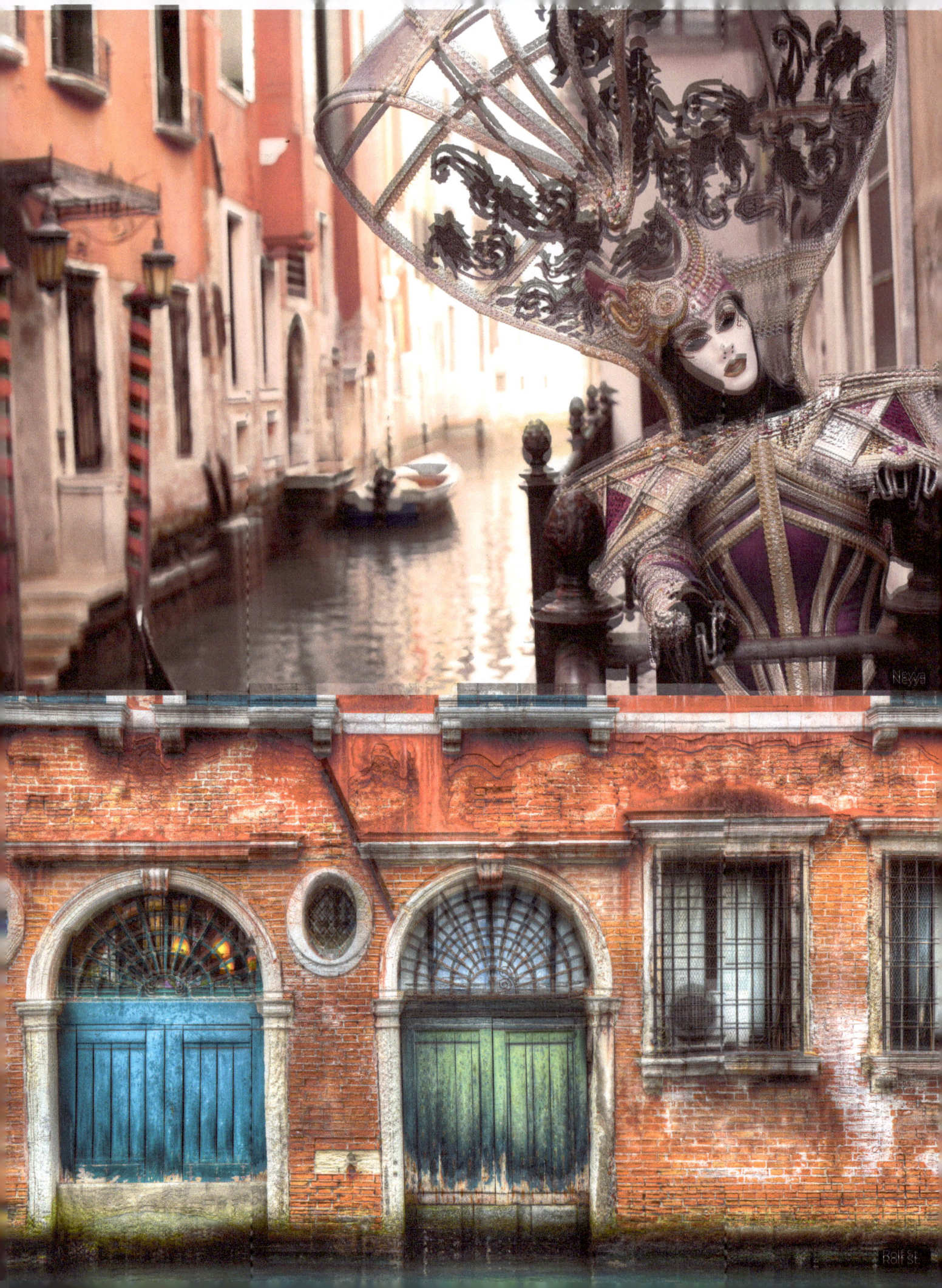

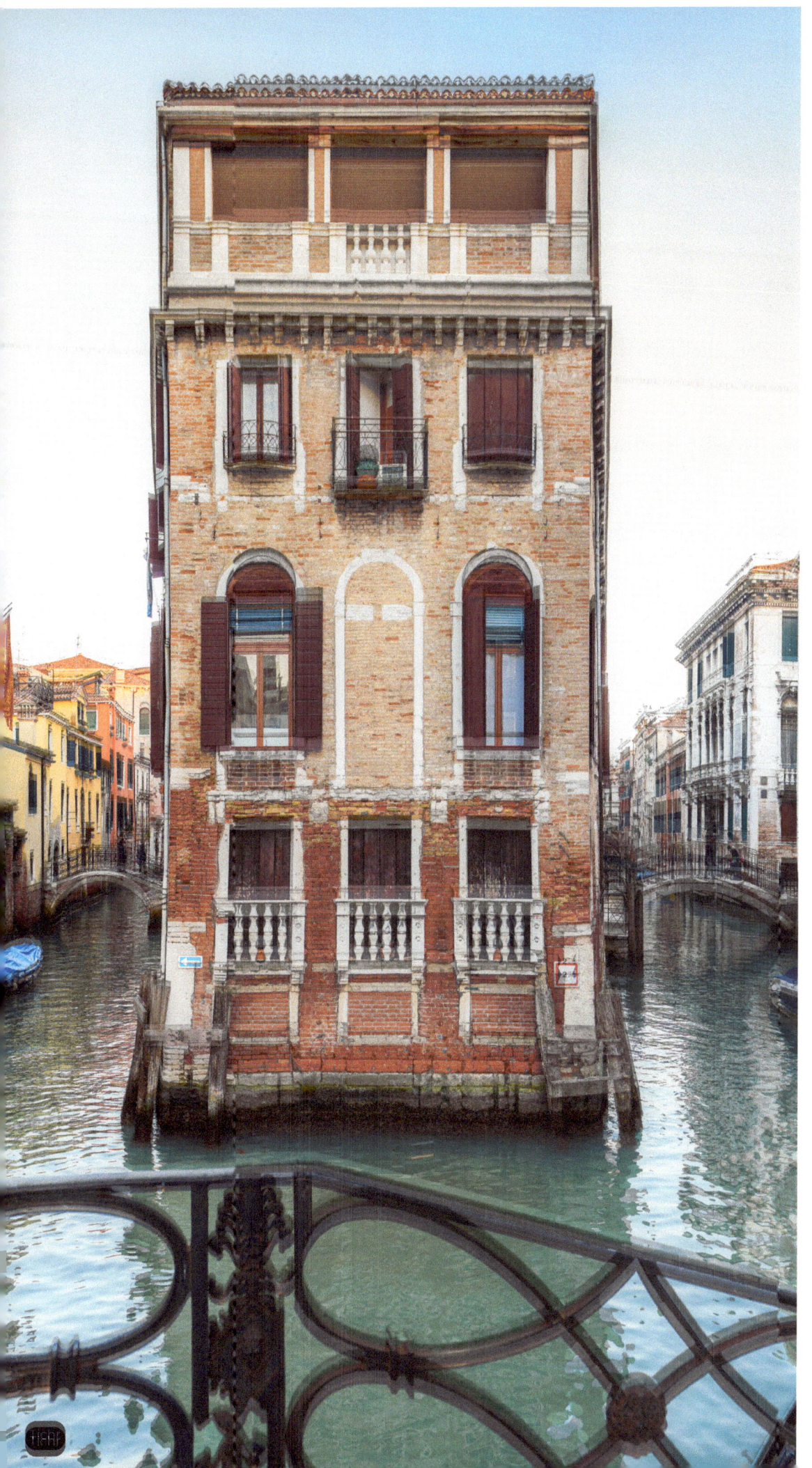

Palazzo Tetta

In "Discovering Venice - La Serenissima Pictorial," we journeyed through the heart of Venice, uncovering the splendor of its landmarks and the stories they hold. Each page was a window into the soul of this enchanting city, revealing its art, history, and enduring charm. For those inspired to delve deeper into the Venetian experience, "UNVEILING VENICE - Your Travel Guide to La Serenissima" is the perfect companion. This guide invites you to discover new facets of Venice's beauty and hidden attractions, enriching your exploration of a city that continually captivates and surprises. Embrace the journey and let Venice reveal its secrets to you.

UNVEILING VENICE

Your Travel Guide to La Serenissima

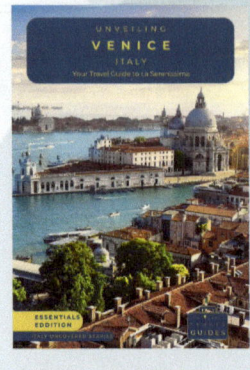

CHECK OUT THE FRANCE UNVEILED TRAVEL GUIDES SERIES

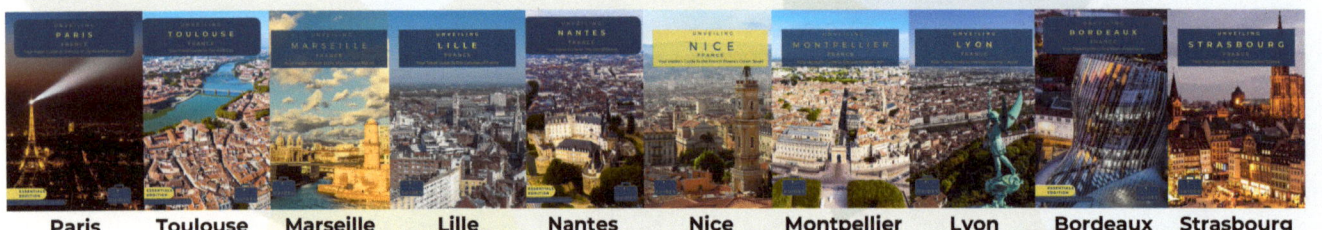

Paris | Toulouse | Marseille | Lille | Nantes | Nice | Montpellier | Lyon | Bordeaux | Strasbourg

CHECK OUT THE ITALY UNCOVERED TRAVEL GUIDES SERIES

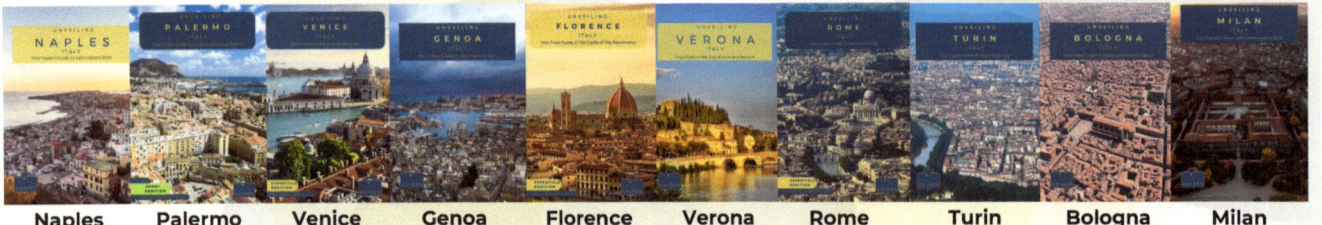

Naples | Palermo | Venice | Genoa | Florence | Verona | Rome | Turin | Bologna | Milan

CHECK OUT THE SPAIN UNVEILED TRAVEL GUIDES SERIES

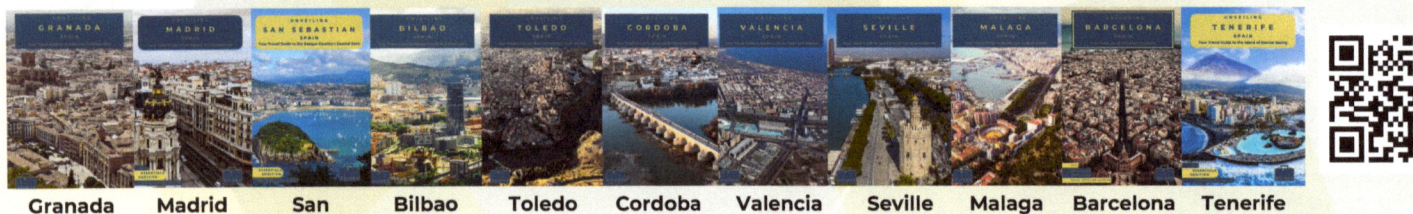

Granada | Madrid | San Sebastian | Bilbao | Toledo | Cordoba | Valencia | Seville | Malaga | Barcelona | Tenerife

Join our Tailored Travel Guides Network for more benefits by accessing this link:
https://mailchi.mp/d151cba349e8/ttgnetwork
Or by scanning the QR code

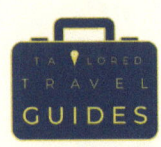

Discover your journey!